REAL ESTATE FINANCING OPTIONS

Adv. Darsh Dharod

Dr. Harshul Savla, D.Litt

INDIA • SINGAPORE • MALAYSIA

ISBN
Paperback 979-8-89699-953-9
Hardcase 979-8-89724-922-0

CONTENTS

About the Author

Adv. Darsh Rekha Ketan Dharod

Adv. Darsh Rekha Ketan Dharod is a young millennial of 28 years having keen interest and plethora of knowledge about the Real Estate Industry.

Adv. Darsh has been keenly watching and tracking the real estate industry from about when he was in his pre-teens, the spark and interest kicked-off in him while visiting a few under construction projects and subsequent interactions with key stakeholders and stalwarts from the industry.

Adv. Darsh is an alumnus of Bombay Scottish School, Mahim an institution which is 176 years old, ranked among the top 2 in Mumbai and top 6 in India. He stood among the top 1 percent in the ICSE Board 10th Grade examinations.

Adv. Darsh has degrees in Accountancy, Finance, Management and Law having studied Bachelors of Accountancy and Finance (B.A.F) from H.R. College of Commerce and Economics in which he stood at 6th Rank in entire University of Mumbai, Bachelors of Law (LL.B) from K.C. Law College, Masters of Commerce in Management (M.Com) and Masters of Law (LL.M) from University of Mumbai and is currently in the last and final stage of completing Chartered Accountancy (CA) from Institute of Chartered Accountants of India and Chartered Financial Analyst (CFA) from CFA Institute, USA.

Adv. Darsh started working rather at an early age of 19 years while still in college, managing both studies and work which has helped him work in different industries.

Adv. Darsh as part of Chartered Accountancy course has completed 3 years of articleship, there after worked in Tata Capital, a Tata Group Company in Special Projects developing a new digitally enabled platform driving collaboration among its business enabling the dream of 'One Tata' which eventually took the shape as the super app 'Tata Neu'. He later worked at HDFC Property Ventures a Real Estate Private Equity Fund and a HDFC Group Company and IEG Investment Banking Group, a German based Investment Bank. He has also worked at Colliers International in their Consulting and Advisory team, in which he advised on various

Real Estate Developments and Asset classes to top Developers, Industrialists and Governments in 25 cities across 7 States and 2 UTs in India.

In his stint at Adani Realty, in CEOs Office- Strategic Projects, he was part of the founding member team for Dharavi Redevelopment Project which is Asia's Largest Slum Rehabilitation and Urban Regeneration Project. Currently, in Godrej Properties, he is a part of the Business Development, Investments and Acquisition team, responsible for acquiring new greenfield and brownfield projects for Godrej Properties in form of Land acquisitions, Strategic Investments and Redevelopment opportunities.

Adv. Darsh has been recipient of many prestigious awards in his life such as the "R.K. Sharma Memorial Prize" for highest distinction in ICSE Examinations, Letter of Appreciation from Mr. Rajendra Darda, Editor in-chief Lokmat and Minister of School Education in Government of Maharashtra. He was felicitated with various awards during his college years for his contribution to college and academic performance by Dr. Indu Shahani, Principal of H.R. College of Commerce and Economics and former Sheriff of Mumbai. He's also been recipient of awards by Bombay Scottish School, K.C. Law College, KVO, LNMA among many others.

Adv. Darsh is actively involved and one of the youngest committee members in the history of CREDAI MCHI (Confederation of Real Estate Developers' Association of India & Maharashtra Chamber of Housing Industry), where he is a part of Statistics and Research Wing. CREDAI MCHI has more than 1800 Developers as its members across 14 City Chapters making up for entire Mumbai Metropolitan Region.

Adv. Darsh is also actively involved and is also one of the youngest committee members in the history of CREDAI National Youth Wing, where he is a part of Business Process Automation Committee. CREDAI National has more than 13,300 Developers as its members in 21 States and 230 City Chapters across India.

Adv. Darsh is also an International Best Selling Author and has authored more than a dozen books on the Real Estate Sector, making his books one of India's and perhaps the World's most comprehensive literatures on Real Estate Sector. Some of his books are: Self Redevelopment & Reviving Stalled Projects, Alternative Real Estate, Insolvency & Bankruptcy Code, Judicial Journey under RERA, ERA post RERA, Funding Options for Developers, FSI- A Development Control Tool, The Redevelopment Guide, etc. The books are available in countries such as but not limited to Singapore, Australia, UK, Canada, Japan, UAE, Germany among many others. The books are available on online portals such as Amazon, Flipkart, Rakuten Kobo, Apple iBooks, Google Play Books, Amazon Kindle, Notion Press across several countries.

Adv. Darsh due to his rich and diversified academic and professional experience, regularly holds Seminars and is also a Guest Lecturer on different topics covering Finance, Law, Real Estate, among others at prestigious colleges in India. He has also written articles and snippets for a few newspapers, magazines and journals.

Adv. Darsh has mentored over 50 students pursuing their Masters, MBA and other specialization courses from institutions and universities such as NMIMS, IIT- Kharagpur, CEPT, NICMAR, RICS, GLC, MIT, UC Berkley, Cranfield, HSNC, Nirma, KC law, Amity among others. Adv. Darsh has also been the guide for final year Dissertation, Thesis, DRP for many of the above students.

Adv. Darsh is also a podcaster, and has hosted and interviewed few of the top experts from the Real Estate Industry through the podcasts, specifically, he has been a host in the Podcast series "The Deep Dive" by CREDAI National which is available across mediums such as Youtube and Spotify, focussing on deep diving into some key aspects related to the real estate industry in India

Adv. Darsh is also actively involved in a few NGOs and for his contributions to society has been facilitated by Ministry of Railways, Government of India among many other organizations. He has also represented India at an UNESCO event held in Europe and Turkey.

Adv. Darsh has keen interest in sports, has run several marathons and been a gold medalist in Swimming, Chess and Badminton.

About the Author

Dr. Harshul Savla, D.Litt.

Dr. Harshul Savla, D.Litt. is Managing Partner of Suvidha Lifespaces which has successfully completed more than 2 million sq.ft. in last 35 years across Mumbai City under the able leadership of Mr. Pramesh Rambhiya. CRISIL India and Realty Icon Awards recognized Dr. Harshul as "Young Thought Leader" and Realty NXT featured him as "Young Turk of Real Estate Sector". He has won the prestigious CREDAI-MCHI Golden Pillar Award in the category of Best Debutant Real Estate Developer and has been awarded "Young Achiever of the Year" by ET NOW, CNN News 18, ZEE

Business, MAHARASHTRA Times, ABP News, Realty+, MID DAY, Business World and Realty Quarter.

Dr. Harshul has featured in the Business World and Realty Plus "40 under 40" list as Real Estate's Young Turk consecutively in 2021, 2022, 2023 and 2024. He has also been awarded the prestigious "Pillars of Maharashtra" award in 2022 by Hon'ble Member of Parliament for Mumbai North. The Times Group's Economic Times has awarded Dr. Harshul Savla as an Inspiring Personality 2022 for exceptional contribution to Real Estate Sector. Mid Day's "Success Stories 2022" has featured Dr. Harshul's various achievements and journey. He has been a TEDx Speaker too.

Dr. Harshul has worked as EA to Ramesh Nair, former Chairman, JLL India and has worked in the Wealth Management Team at TATA Capital where he was awarded the National Award for Exemplary Performance. He is a perfect blend of Corporate Experience along with stellar education credentials of Ph.D., LL.M, LL.B, MBA and BMS from prestigious institutions like JBIMS, GLC, NM and Department of Law, University of Mumbai.

Dr. Harshul holds the World Record for "Maximum Degree from Single University" and his World Record is mentioned in World Book of Records London, The British World Records, International Book of Records, International Talent Book of Records, Exclusive World Record, Asian World Records, Global Records & Research Foundation, Amazing Indian Records, World Records India, India Book of Records, Kohinoor Vidyasamrat, Champion Book of World Record, High Range Book of World Records etc.

He also holds the World Record for "Maximum Books Authored & Published in a Year" for authoring and publishing 12 Real Estate Books in the year 2021 in English Language. Dr. Harshul is awarded as "Author of the Year" at the prestigious CNBC Awaaz Real Estate Excellence Awards 2022 held at Taj Lands End, Mumbai.

Dr. Harshul was awarded Doctorate (Ph.D.) for his Thesis on REITs (Real Estate Investment Trusts) which is first such thesis in India on the said subject and the Thesis is also available in the form of a book. Apart from this he is an NSE Certified Market Professional - Level 4 and has done a course on 'Strategic Real Estate Management' from ISB, Hyderabad.

Dr. Harshul is "Chairman: Statistics & Standards" at CREDAI National, which has more than 13,300 Real Estate Developers as its Members and has presence in 230 Cities (21 State Chapters). He is Research Convenor of CREDAI MCHI and heads its Statistics & Research Wing. CREDAI MCHI is a leading Real Estate Developers Association of MMR having 1,800 members across its 14 Units. Dr. Harshul has also served as the National Head of the Committee on E-Learning and Masterclass at CREDAI National Youth Wing from 2021-2023 and is presently the "Chairman: Business Process Optimization"

Dr. Harshul is also an Amazon Best Selling Author and has authored 22 books on the Real Estate Sector and General Management, making his books one of India's most comprehensive literatures on Real Estate Sector. Some of his books are: Real Estate Laws, Reality of Realty, Real Estate Valuation, Affordable Housing, NBFC & HFC Crisis, Fractional Ownership & REITs, Insolvency & Bankruptcy Code, Self-Redevelopment & Reviving Stalled Projects, Digitalizing Real Estate Sector in Built Environment, Building Information Modeling, Green Buildings, Facility Management, COVID-O-NOMICS, Luxury Retail, Alternative Real Estate, Judicial Journey under RERA, Self-Redevelopment and Reviving Stalled Projects, NCLT & IBC in Real Estate Sector, ERA POST RERA, Funding

Options for Developers, FSI – A Development Control Tool, The Redevelopment Guide, RERA Simplified etc. He regularly writes articles for fortnightly business magazine "Property House" and may other newspapers and journals.

Dr. Harshul is Associate Professor at ITM University and is also a Ph.D. Guide / Supervisor with them. He was a Visiting Faculty and Guest Lecturer at the prestigious RICS School of Built Environment, Mumbai Campus. He taught the subject 'Real Estate Development Process' to Management Students at the Mumbai Campus. He was also a Guest Lecturer at REMI - The Real Estate Management Institute, Mumbai. He was Invited to conduct Session on REITs in India for Developers Members of NAREDCO and was one of the youngest Member Developer to do so. He has also delivered a lecture at PEATA (I) on Future of Realty. He is also a renowned moderator for panels discussing various aspects of Realty and has moderated more than 60 panel discussions so far.

Dr. Harshul has recently embarked his research journey for his second Ph.D. which he is pursuing from the Department of Law, University of Mumbai under the guidance of Former HOD of the Department. His thesis is on the topic of RERA and will be the first Ph.D. in Law thesis in India on RERA.

Dr. Harshul is also the Founding Member of the "RERA Practitioners' Welfare Association" and the Founding Member of "IRIYA Realty Intelligentsia and Advisory Foundation of India" which comprises of Innovation Centre, Think Tank and Centre of Excellence. Dr. Harshul is also part of the Managing Committee of IBG (India Business Group). Dr. Harshul is a Founding Member at the 500 MBA Club and also a Mentor at the Founder Institute which is the world's most proven network to turn ideas into fundable startups and startups into global businesses.

Research Associate

Amaanuddin Siddique

Amaan Siddique is a 20-year-old student with a profound interest in real estate. He achieved remarkable academic success at Beacon High School, Mumbai, where he served as head boy, scoring 99% in his ICSE examinations and 96% in his ISC examinations at Jasudben ML School. Currently, he is pursuing a degree in Statistics and Economics at St. Xavier's College, Mumbai, which is recognized as the number one autonomous college in India. This prestigious institution is renowned for its rigorous academic standards, holistic education approach, and strong emphasis on research and extracurricular activities.

Amaan's passion for the real estate industry stems from his early exposure to it through his father, Moinuddin Siddique, who is the founder of Doors Realty, a company renowned for its consultation in luxury real estate in Mumbai. He has also gained valuable insights from his maternal uncle, Naveen Nandwani, Managing Director at Savills. Working alongside his father has provided Amaan with invaluable experiences, deepening his love for the industry. He wishes to work in real estate moving forward and hopes to bring about positive changes by leveraging his diverse academic knowledge and industry experience. He has also had the privilege of learning from esteemed professionals such as Dr. Adv. Harshul Savla, which has further deepened his appreciation for the field.

In addition to his academic and professional pursuits, Amaan is an active social advocate, involved with NGOs that focus on environmental conservation. He has participated in significant initiatives, including protests to protect Aarey Forest. Amaan also has a keen interest in sports and fitness, having played cricket at a professional level, and he is dedicated to maintaining a healthy lifestyle. In his leisure time, he enjoys wildlife photography, capturing the beauty of nature.

Research Acknowledgements

- CA Aniket Bagve – Founder, MYCAP Advisors
- Harshal Trivedi – Director, Kutir Group
- Hirvita Desai – Founding Partner, FYG Advisory
- Jay Kapadia – Chief Manager, MD's Office, Paradigm Realty
- Laxminarayan Ranga – Founding Partner, FYG Advisory
- Priyank Shah – Real Estate Private Equity
- Shirin Gwalani
- Siddhi More – Savills, Middle East

Part 1

REAL ESTATE FINANCE

Overview of Real Estate Finance

Definition and Importance

Real estate project finance refers to the provision of capital required to fund various stages of a real estate development, ensuring that the running costs of a new project are covered through strategic financial planning. This financing is typically structured over the asset's life, combining both debt and equity. The approach to financing evolves throughout the life cycle of the project, with each stage requiring a distinct strategy based on the current state of the development and the associated risks. In the early phases, equity financing is often preferred due to its lower risk and greater accessibility compared to traditional bank loans. As the project matures and risks become more manageable, debt financing becomes a more viable option.

Real estate project finance utilizes a variety of financial tools, each with its unique advantages and disadvantages. These include debt instruments such as non-convertible debentures, bank loans, and external commercial borrowings, which provide the necessary capital with the obligation of repayment. Equity financing options, including investments from family offices, institutional funds, and foreign direct investment (FDI), offer ownership stakes in the project in exchange for capital. Additionally, real estate projects can be funded through asset-class instruments such as infrastructure investment trusts (INVITs) and real estate investment trusts (REITs), which pool capital from multiple investors. Another specialized tool, lease rental discounting (LRD), allows developers to raise funds based on future rental income from leased properties. Together, these diverse financing strategies enable developers to secure the necessary capital throughout the project's life cycle, from inception to completion.

Overview of Stakeholders

Real estate finance involves several key stakeholders, each playing a unique role in the capital provision and management:

Developers: They require capital at various stages of the project lifecycle, from land acquisition to the construction and sale of properties.

Investors: Ranging from individual buyers to institutional investors, their goal is to earn returns through capital appreciation or rental income.

Financial Institutions: Banks, NBFCs, and private equity firms evaluate and provide funding to real estate projects.

Homebuyers: In residential projects, they contribute significantly to financing through down payments and mortgages, while also driving demand.

Structure of Financing

Real estate project financing typically combines the following structures:

- **Debt Financing:** Involves borrowing capital that must be repaid with interest. Common instruments include bank loans, syndicated loans, non-convertible debentures, and external commercial borrowings.
- **Equity Financing:** Involves raising capital by offering ownership stakes in the project. This may include private equity, joint ventures, or institutional investments.
- **Hybrid Structures:** These combine both debt and equity, optimizing returns and balancing risk for stakeholders.
- **Specialized Financing:** This includes tools such as lease rental discounting, real estate crowdfunding, and government subsidies aimed at specific project types.

Real Estate Project Financing Tools

Debt Financing

- **Bank Loans:** Long-term loans from traditional financial institutions, typically with lower interest rates and stricter conditions.
- **Private Equity/Venture Capital (PE/VC):** Debt-like investments from private investors or firms, focusing on high-risk, high-reward projects.
- **Syndicated Loans:** A group of lenders providing large-scale loans, sharing the risk and interest.

- **Non-Convertible Debentures (NCDs):** Long-term instruments raised through public or private issues offering fixed returns, categorized as secured or unsecured.
- **External Commercial Borrowings (ECBs):** Funds raised from foreign markets for large-scale projects, subject to compliance with FEMA regulations.
- **Hard Money Loans:** Short-term, high-interest loans secured by the real estate property itself.

Equity Financing

- **Equity Investments:** Investors provide capital in exchange for ownership stakes, sharing in both risks and rewards.
- **Joint Ventures (JVs):** Partnerships where risks and profits are shared between developers and investors, often used in large-scale projects.
- **Private Equity:** Investments from private individuals or institutional funds, typically seeking higher returns in exchange for assuming more risk.
- **Preferred Equity:** Investment with fixed returns and priority payouts over common equity holders, offering a balance of risk and return.

Foreign Direct Investment (FDI)

- **Investments from foreign entities**: These are direct investments made by foreign firms or individuals in real estate projects within the host country, often in the form of purchasing land or properties.

Government Programs and Subsidies

- **Tax Increment Financing (TIF):** A financing tool where future tax revenues generated by a project are used to fund its development.
- **Low-Income Housing Tax Credits (LIHTC):** Tax incentives given to developers of affordable housing projects to encourage their development.
- **Grants and Subsidies:** Government-provided financial aid aimed at promoting sustainable or affordable real estate projects.

Specialized Financing

- **Real Estate Crowdfunding:** Online platforms allowing multiple small investors to pool funds to finance real estate projects.
- **Syndication:** A group investment model where a lead sponsor manages the investment, sharing profits among participants.
- **Seller Financing:** Property owners act as lenders to buyers, offering loans directly for property transactions.
- **Opportunity Zone Investments:** Tax benefits granted to projects located in designated economically distressed areas, encouraging development in these zones.

Tax and Accounting Tools

- **Tax Abatements:** Property tax reductions offered to developers to incentivize development in certain areas.
- **Depreciation and Tax Shield:** The tax benefits developers and investors receive from depreciating the value of real estate over time, reducing taxable income.

Part 2

Regulatory Framework for Real Estate

Pre-RERA vs. Post-RERA Era

The Real Estate (Regulation and Development) Act, commonly known as RERA, has brought significant changes to the real estate sector. This section compares the practices prevalent in the pre-RERA era with those established under RERA guidelines, enabling buyers and developers to make informed decisions in today's real estate market.

Transparency and Accountability

In the **pre-RERA** era, developers often engaged in ambiguous practices, such as misleading advertisements, delayed project deliveries, and unexplained changes in project specifications. Buyers had limited access to credible information about projects, leading to mistrust and confusion.

Under RERA:

- Developers must register their projects with the state-specific RERA authority before advertising or selling them.
- They are required to provide precise project details, including layout plans, amenities, construction progress, and completion timelines.

- Regular updates must be shared via state RERA websites, ensuring real-time transparency.

This empowers buyers to make informed decisions and holds developers accountable for their commitments.

Buyer Protection

In the **pre-RERA** era, buyers faced challenges such as one-sided contracts, unfair clauses, and inadequate dispute resolution mechanisms. Funds collected from buyers were often diverted to other projects, leaving buyers financially vulnerable.

Under RERA:

- Buyers have access to all relevant project information, including the builder's track record, necessary approvals, and financial statements.
- Developers must deposit 70% of the funds collected into an escrow account, ensuring the money is used exclusively for the designated project.
- Legal safeguards now provide buyers with protection against fraudulent practices, enhancing confidence in the market.

Timely Project Delivery

Delays in project completion were rampant **pre-RERA**, causing financial and emotional distress to homebuyers. Developers often faced no penalties for missed deadlines, further aggravating buyer concerns.

Under RERA:

- Developers must register projects with a clearly defined timeline for completion.

- Any delay results in penalties or compensation to affected buyers.
- For instance, failure to meet deadlines can lead to fines and even suspension of project registration.

This ensures accountability and significantly reduces project delays.

Dispute Resolution Mechanism

Pre-RERA, buyers had limited recourse in resolving disputes. The absence of a centralized or reliable dispute resolution mechanism left them at a disadvantage.

Under RERA:

- Each state now has a **dedicated Real Estate Regulatory Authority** to handle disputes and grievances.
- Buyers can raise complaints against developers for non-compliance, ensuring **fair and speedy resolution**.
- Developers are also given the opportunity to resolve disputes transparently.

This streamlined mechanism fosters trust between buyers and developers.

Pre-RERA vs. Post-RERA: At a Glance

Aspect	Pre-RERA	Post-RERA (RERA Guidelines)
Transparency	Misleading ads, ambiguous practices	Accurate details, mandatory registration, real-time updates

Buyer Protection	One-sided contracts, limited recourse	Legal safeguards, escrow accounts, comprehensive disclosures
Timely Delivery	Frequent delays, no penalties for developers	Strict timelines, penalties for non-compliance
Dispute Resolution	Lengthy, unreliable mechanisms	Dedicated authorities for quick grievance redressal

Challenges in Implementation

While RERA has transformed the real estate sector, its implementation varies across states. Some states are still working towards robust enforcement, and initial resistance from developers to adopt stringent guidelines remains a challenge.

The Final Word

RERA has ushered in a new era of transparency, accountability, and buyer protection in the real estate industry. Buyers now benefit from access to credible information, timely project completion, and a reliable dispute resolution mechanism. Developers, in turn, enjoy a streamlined process, enhanced market credibility, and increased consumer trust. Despite implementation challenges, RERA's impact on stabilizing the real estate market and boosting consumer confidence is undeniable.

Part 3

Valuation Techniques

Valuation Techniques in Real Estate

Introduction

Valuation is a cornerstone of real estate finance, providing a reliable estimate of property value. Accurate valuation is critical for developers, investors, lenders, and buyers, as it forms the basis for decision-making in transactions, investments, taxation, and financing. Various valuation techniques are employed to suit the diverse nature of properties and their intended purposes. This chapter delves into the most widely used valuation methods and their applications.

Market Comparison Approach

The **Market Comparison Approach (MCA)** is a direct and widely used valuation method. It determines a property's value by comparing it to similar properties that have recently been sold in the same location.

Key Features:

1. **Comparable Sales Data:** This approach relies on recent sales of properties with similar characteristics, such as size, age, location, and amenities.
2. **Adjustments for Differences:** Adjustments are made for factors such as renovations, location premiums, or differing lot sizes to arrive at a more accurate value.
3. **Applicability:** MCA is especially effective for residential properties and other markets where comparable transactions are available.

Advantages:

- Easy to understand and apply when sufficient data is available.
- Reflects current market conditions.

Challenges:

- Limited applicability for unique or specialized properties.
- Requires up-to-date and accurate sales data.

Example:

A 1,500 sq. ft. apartment in a metropolitan area is being valued. Recent sales in the area include:

- **Property A:** Sold for ₹1.5 crore, similar size and amenities.
- **Property B:** Sold for ₹1.7 crore but with a premium location and additional parking space.

Adjustments are made to reflect differences, and the subject property's value is estimated at ₹1.6 crore.

Income Capitalization Approach

The **Income Capitalization Approach** is widely used for valuing income-generating properties such as commercial buildings, rental apartments, and office spaces. This method estimates a property's value based on its ability to generate future income.

Key Concepts:

1. **Net Operating Income (NOI):** The property's annual income after operating expenses but before debt service and taxes.
2. **Capitalization Rate (Cap Rate):** The rate of return expected by investors, influenced by market conditions, property type, and risk factors.

Applicability:

- Best suited for stabilized properties with predictable income streams.
- Commonly used by investors and appraisers for commercial real estate.

Advantages:

- Provides a clear picture of income potential.
- Simple and straightforward for stable properties.

Challenges:

- Less accurate for properties with fluctuating income.
- Cap rates may vary widely across markets.

Example:

A retail property generates an NOI of ₹50 lakh annually, and the market cap rate is 8%. Using the formula:

Value = ₹50,00,00/0.08 = ₹6.25 Cr

Cost Approach

The **Cost Approach** evaluates a property's value based on the cost of reproducing or replacing it, minus depreciation, and adding the land value.

Key Features:

1. **Replacement/Reproduction Cost:** The expense required to rebuild the property at current prices.
2. **Depreciation Adjustment:** Accounts for physical wear and tear, functional obsolescence, and economic factors.
3. **Land Value:** Estimated separately using market data.

Applicability:

- Ideal for new constructions or unique properties where comparable data is unavailable.
- Frequently used for insurance purposes.

Advantages:

- Reliable for properties with limited market comparisons.
- Useful for evaluating rebuild costs.

Challenges:

- Depreciation estimates can be subjective.
- Does not account for current market demand.

Example:

A factory has a replacement cost of ₹10 crore. Accounting for depreciation at ₹2 crore, and adding the land value of ₹3 crore:

Value = ₹10 Cr - ₹2 Cr + ₹3 Cr = ₹11 Cr

Discounted Cash Flow (DCF) Method

The **Discounted Cash Flow (DCF) Method** is a comprehensive technique that evaluates a property's value by projecting future cash flows and discounting them to present value.

Key Concepts:

1. **Future Cash Flows:** Includes rental income, operating expenses, and sale proceeds at the end of the holding period.
2. **Discount Rate:** Reflects the time value of money and investment risk.

Applicability:

- Suited for complex projects with variable income streams.
- Commonly used in feasibility studies for new developments.

Advantages:

- Captures both income and appreciation potential.
- Highly customizable based on project specifics.

Challenges:

- Requires accurate forecasting and assumptions.
- Sensitive to changes in discount rates.

Example:

A commercial property generates cash flows of ₹10 lakh annually for 5 years, with a terminal value of ₹1 crore in Year 5. At a discount rate of 10%, the present value is calculated for each cash flow, yielding a total value of ₹1.18 crore.

Valuation of Mixed-Use and Specialized Properties

Mixed-use and specialized properties, such as hotels, hospitals, and industrial facilities, require tailored valuation approaches due to their unique characteristics.

Key Features:

1. **Component Valuation:** For mixed-use properties, individual components (residential, retail, commercial) are valued separately.
2. **Industry-Specific Metrics:** Metrics like occupancy rates, Average Daily Rate (ADR) for hotels, or throughput for industrial facilities are factored into valuation.

Applicability:

Necessary for properties with diverse income streams or operational complexities.

Advantages:

Provides a nuanced view of value for complex properties.

Challenges:

Requires specialized knowledge and data.

Example:

A mixed-use property has three components: retail (₹5 crore), residential (₹3 crore), and office (₹4 crore). The total value is the sum of the individual valuations, equalling ₹12 crore.

Hybrid Valuation Approaches

Hybrid valuation techniques combine multiple methods to provide a more comprehensive and reliable estimate, especially for complex or mixed-use properties.

Key Features:

1. **Blended Methodology:** Combines market comparison, income capitalization, and cost approaches based on the property's characteristics.
2. **Weighted Valuation:** Assigns weights to each method depending on its relevance to the property.

Applicability:

- Used for complex assets where no single approach offers a complete picture.
- Effective for large projects combining commercial, residential, and industrial components.

Advantages:

- Offers flexibility and a balanced view.
- Reduces biases associated with individual techniques.

Challenges:

Requires expertise to determine appropriate weights and ensure consistency.

Example:

For a large mixed-use property with residential and commercial elements, 40% weight is assigned to the income capitalization approach, 30% to the market comparison approach, and 30% to the cost approach. The final value is a weighted average of the results from each method.

Automated Valuation Models (AVMs)

Automated Valuation Models (AVMs) are technology-driven tools that leverage data analytics, algorithms, and machine learning to estimate property values.

Key Features:

1. **Data-Driven Analysis:** Utilizes historical data, market trends, and comparable sales.
2. **Rapid Processing:** Provides near-instant valuations with minimal human intervention.
3. **Standardization:** Reduces subjectivity in valuation by relying on consistent algorithms.

Applicability:

- Frequently used by banks, real estate platforms, and government agencies for preliminary assessments.
- Effective for high-volume, standardized properties like residential units.

Advantages:

- Cost-effective and time-efficient.
- Ideal for markets with abundant data.

Challenges:

- Limited accuracy for unique or specialized properties.
- Relies heavily on the quality and availability of data.

Example:

An AVM might use algorithms to estimate the value of a 3-bedroom apartment in Mumbai based on recent sales in the locality, property age, and other parameters, yielding a valuation of ₹2 crore.

Specialized Approaches for Complex Properties

While traditional valuation techniques such as the Market Comparison, Income Capitalization, and Cost Approach are commonly used, certain properties require specialized methods due to their unique characteristics. These methods address the challenges posed by mixed-use developments, heritage properties, and properties in evolving markets.

Valuation of Mixed-Use Properties

Mixed-use developments combine residential, commercial, and recreational spaces within a single project. Valuing such properties requires understanding the interplay of these different components.

- **Separate Component Analysis:** Each component is valued individually using the most appropriate approach (e.g., Income Capitalization for commercial spaces and Market Comparison for residential units). The total value is derived by aggregating these components.

- **Allocation of Common Costs:** Shared amenities such as parking spaces, green areas, and infrastructure must be apportioned based on usage or contribution to revenue streams.
- **Weighted Average Valuation:** In cases where components are interdependent, a weighted average of their values may be used to reflect overall project viability.

Valuation of Specialized Properties

Specialized properties, such as hotels, hospitals, and industrial facilities, require bespoke valuation techniques due to their reliance on specific operational and market factors.

- **Hotels:**

  Valuation focuses on income generated from room tariffs, food and beverage sales, and events. Key metrics include the Average Daily Rate (ADR) and Revenue per Available Room (RevPAR).

- **Hospitals:**

  Valued based on operational revenue, including patient care, outpatient services, and pharmacy sales. Factors such as patient footfall and medical equipment value are crucial.

- **Industrial Facilities:**

  These properties depend heavily on location, logistical access, and zoning compliance. Valuation considers adaptability for alternative uses and market demand for specific industries.

Valuation in Emerging Markets

Emerging markets present unique challenges due to volatile pricing, inconsistent data, and evolving regulatory frameworks.

- **Trend Analysis:** Historical data is often sparse or unreliable, so valuers rely on trend projections based on market fundamentals like population growth, infrastructure development, and urbanization rates.
- **Scenario Modelling:** Sensitivity analysis is conducted to simulate the impact of varying market conditions on property value.
- **Risk Adjustments:** A premium is added to account for higher uncertainties and potential delays in market maturity.

Who Conducts Real Estate Valuation?

Real estate valuation is a specialized process carried out by trained professionals with expertise in property markets, financial analysis, and legal frameworks. These individuals or organizations play a crucial role in providing accurate and unbiased property assessments.

Key Professionals Involved

1. **Certified Valuers/Appraisers**

   Certified valuers, often accredited by governing bodies or institutions like the Institution of Valuers (IOV) or Royal Institution of Chartered Surveyors (RICS), specialize in property valuation. They are responsible for preparing detailed valuation reports in compliance with local and international standards.

   Role:

   - Conduct site inspections to assess property conditions.
   - Analyse market trends and comparable sales data.

- Prepare valuation reports for clients, lenders, or regulatory authorities.

2. **Chartered Accountants and Financial Analysts**

   These professionals assist in valuing properties for financial reporting, mergers and acquisitions, and tax purposes. They focus on the financial aspects of valuation, such as cash flow projections and return on investment analysis.

   Role:

   - Calculate the Net Present Value (NPV) and Internal Rate of Return (IRR) for income-generating properties.
   - Ensure compliance with accounting standards, such as IFRS or Indian GAAP.

3. **Surveyors and Civil Engineers**

   Surveyors and civil engineers contribute by providing technical evaluations of a property's physical structure, land measurements, and compliance with zoning laws. Their input is critical for cost-based valuation methods.

   Role:

   - Conduct feasibility studies and structural assessments.
   - Evaluate land use and adherence to building codes.

4. **Real Estate Consultants**

   Real estate consultants provide valuation insights based on market expertise. They often collaborate with certified valuers to offer strategic advice to developers, investors, and corporate clients.

Role:

- Advise on optimal pricing strategies for sales or leases.
- Offer insights into future market trends and investment potential.

5. **Bank and Financial Institution Valuers**

   Lenders often have in-house or empanelled valuation experts who assess properties as part of the loan approval process. Their valuations focus on determining collateral value to mitigate lending risks.

   Role:

   - Appraise properties for mortgage underwriting.
   - Ensure compliance with lending norms and risk management practices.

6. **Government and Regulatory Valuers**

   These valuers work for public bodies or regulatory authorities, providing assessments for property taxation, acquisition, or disputes. For example, *district valuation offices* in India assist in determining compensation for land acquisition under the Right to Fair Compensation Act.

   Role:

   - Calculate property taxes and acquisition costs.
   - Act as expert witnesses in legal disputes related to valuation.

Qualifications and Standards

To ensure professionalism and accuracy, valuers are often required to meet specific qualifications and adhere to established standards:

Certifications: Professionals are certified through organizations like RICS, IOV, or the Appraisal Institute.

Regulatory Standards: Valuations must comply with frameworks such as the *International Valuation Standards (IVS)* or country-specific guidelines like those from the *National Institute of Valuers (NIV)* in India.

Ethics and Transparency: Valuers must uphold ethical practices, avoiding conflicts of interest and ensuring impartiality in their assessments.

The Importance of Professional Valuation

The expertise of valuation professionals ensures that stakeholders—whether they are buyers, sellers, lenders, or government authorities—receive reliable and objective property assessments. Professional valuations minimize risks, aid decision-making, and enhance market transparency, fostering trust among all parties involved in real estate transactions.

Regulatory Framework Governing Real Estate Valuation

The valuation of real estate plays a critical role in property transactions, investment decisions, taxation, and compliance with regulatory requirements. To ensure the process is transparent, consistent, and accurate, a robust regulatory framework is essential. In India, this framework is governed by a combination of global standards, national legislation, and industry-specific guidelines. These regulations enhance the credibility of valuations, particularly in transactions involving financial institutions, dispute resolution, and public sector projects. Below is an elaboration of the key regulatory bodies, standards, and obligations that govern real estate valuation in India.

Key Regulatory Bodies and Standards

1. **The Royal Institution of Chartered Surveyors (RICS):**

   The Royal Institution of Chartered Surveyors (RICS) is a globally recognized professional body that sets the "Red Book" valuation standards. These standards emphasize the principles of transparency, accountability, and uniformity, ensuring that valuation practices are reliable and ethical. In India, RICS-certified professionals are often employed for complex valuations, such as large-scale commercial properties, public infrastructure, and high-value residential projects. The standards prescribed by RICS serve as benchmarks for professional conduct and quality in valuation practices.

2. **International Valuation Standards Council (IVSC):**

   The International Valuation Standards Council (IVSC) develops and promotes international valuation standards for assets, including real estate. These standards aim to ensure consistency in valuation practices globally, providing a common framework for financial institutions, regulators, and valuers. IVSC's guidelines are especially significant for cross-border transactions, foreign direct investment (FDI), and multinational real estate projects, helping to bridge regulatory differences between countries.

3. **Institute of Valuers (IOV):**

   The Institute of Valuers (IOV) is one of the leading professional bodies in India, responsible for certifying and regulating valuers. It focuses on establishing best practices in property valuation across diverse categories, such as land, residential buildings, and industrial properties. The IOV also provides training programs, certifications, and continuous professional development to ensure that valuers remain updated with the latest methodologies and regulations.

4. **Companies Act, 2013:**

   The Companies Act, 2013, governs several aspects of corporate functioning, including property valuation. Section 247 of the Act mandates that only registered valuers, recognized by the Insolvency and Bankruptcy Board of India (IBBI), can undertake valuations for compliance purposes. These valuations are required for mergers, acquisitions, liquidation, and other corporate activities. The Act ensures that valuations are conducted by qualified professionals adhering to standardized methodologies, thereby reducing the risk of discrepancies or manipulation.

5. **Real Estate (Regulation and Development) Act, 2016 (RERA):**

   RERA was enacted to bring transparency and accountability to real estate transactions. It mandates the use of independent valuation reports for new projects, ensuring fair pricing and protecting the interests of homebuyers. By requiring developers to disclose the value of assets, RERA helps maintain trust between stakeholders and promotes ethical practices in the real estate market. The Act also holds valuers accountable for the accuracy of their assessments.

6. **Reserve Bank of India (RBI):**

   The Reserve Bank of India (RBI) has established guidelines for property valuations related to banking and financial services. These guidelines govern the valuation of properties offered as collateral for loans, ensuring that banks and financial institutions adhere to standard practices. RBI regulations aim to minimize risks in lending by ensuring that collateral values are accurately assessed, thereby protecting both lenders and borrowers.

Ethical and Legal Obligations of Valuers

Valuers are entrusted with significant responsibilities, as their assessments directly influence financial decisions, regulatory compliance, and public trust. To uphold the integrity of the valuation process, valuers must adhere to ethical and legal standards. Below are the key obligations of valuers in real estate:

1. **Impartiality and Objectivity:**

   Valuers must remain impartial and objective in their assessments. They should avoid conflicts of interest, such as situations where they have a financial stake in the property being valued or personal ties to the client. Maintaining independence ensures that valuations are unbiased and credible. For instance, a valuer assessing a property for a bank loan must not be influenced by the client's preferences or the bank's expectations.

2. **Confidentiality:**

   Valuers are often privy to sensitive financial and property-related information. They are obligated to handle such data securely and ensure it is shared only with authorized stakeholders. For example, a valuer conducting a valuation for a corporate acquisition must ensure that details of the transaction are not disclosed prematurely. Breaching confidentiality can lead to reputational damage and legal consequences.

3. **Legal Compliance:**

   Valuers must comply with local laws and regulations, including zoning restrictions, building codes, environmental standards, and taxation statutes. For example, when valuing a commercial property, a valuer must consider whether the property adheres to zoning laws and regulatory approvals. Failing to account for these factors could result in inaccurate valuations and potential legal disputes.

4. **Accountability:**

   Valuers are accountable for the accuracy of their assessments. Incorrect or biased valuations can lead to significant financial losses for stakeholders and legal penalties for the valuer. For instance, overvaluing a property in a mortgage transaction could result in loan defaults, while undervaluing a property could lead to disputes and dissatisfaction among clients.

Part 4

Insurance in Real Estate

Real Estate Insurance in India

Introduction

Real estate insurance is a fundamental component of the real estate ecosystem, serving as a critical risk management tool for property owners, developers, investors, and homebuyers. It provides financial protection against unforeseen events that could result in significant losses, ensuring the stability and continuity of real estate projects and investments. By mitigating risks such as natural disasters, accidents, theft, and legal disputes, real estate insurance not only safeguards the value of properties but also enhances market confidence and facilitates smoother transactions.

This chapter delves into the various aspects of real estate insurance, including its key types, the roles of different stakeholders, the regulatory framework governing insurance practices, and the specific insurance needs of developers and homebuyers. Additionally, it explores the importance of real estate insurance and the challenges faced in the industry.

Key Types of Real Estate Insurance

Real estate insurance encompasses a broad spectrum of policies tailored to address different risks associated with property ownership and development. Understanding these types is essential for stakeholders to select the appropriate coverage based on their specific needs.

1. Property Insurance

Property insurance is one of the most common forms of real estate insurance, providing coverage for physical assets such as buildings, fixtures, and equipment against risks like fire, theft, vandalism, and natural disasters.

Coverage Includes:

- Structural damage to the building.
- Loss or damage to personal property within the building.
- Costs associated with repairs or reconstruction.

2. Title Insurance

Title insurance protects property buyers and lenders from financial losses arising from defects in the title, such as legal disputes, fraud, or undisclosed claims. It ensures that the buyer has a clear and marketable title to the property.

Coverage Includes:

- Legal fees for defending the title.
- Financial losses due to title defects.

Example: If a previously unknown lien is discovered on a property after purchase, title insurance covers the associated legal and financial costs, protecting the buyer from potential losses.

3. Liability Insurance

Liability insurance shields property owners from claims resulting from injuries or accidents that occur on their premises. This is particularly important for commercial properties where the risk of accidents involving employees, customers, or visitors is higher.

Coverage Includes:

- Medical expenses for injured parties.
- Legal fees and settlements related to lawsuits.

4. Business Interruption Insurance

Business interruption insurance compensates property owners or businesses for income lost due to events that disrupt operations, such as fires, floods, or other insured risks. This coverage ensures financial stability during periods of inactivity caused by unforeseen events.

Coverage Includes:

- Lost revenue during the interruption.
- Ongoing expenses like rent and utilities.
- Costs associated with restoring operations.

5. Construction Insurance

Also known as builder's risk insurance, construction insurance covers risks associated with construction projects. It provides coverage for damages to the project site, equipment, and materials due to events like accidents, theft, or natural disasters.

Coverage Includes:

- Damage to partially constructed buildings.
- Loss of construction materials.
- Equipment breakdowns.

6. Mortgage Insurance

Mortgage insurance protects lenders from losses in case borrowers default on their loans. This insurance is typically required when borrowers make a down payment that is less than a certain percentage of the property's value.

Coverage Includes:

- Compensation to lenders for losses due to borrower default.
- Coverage based on the loan amount and borrower's creditworthiness.

7. Flood and Earthquake Insurance

Standard property insurance policies often exclude coverage for natural calamities like floods and earthquakes. Separate flood or earthquake insurance policies are available to cover these specific risks, protecting properties located in high-risk areas.

Coverage Includes:

- Structural damage caused by floods or earthquakes.
- Replacement costs for damaged property.

Key Players in Real Estate Insurance

The real estate insurance landscape involves various stakeholders, each playing a distinct role in providing and managing insurance coverage for properties.

1. Insurance Companies

Major insurance companies offer a variety of policies tailored to real estate needs, including general property insurance, liability coverage, and title insurance. They assess risks, determine premiums, and provide financial compensation in the event of a claim.

Role:

- Develop and underwrite insurance policies.
- Assess and manage risks associated with property insurance.
- Process claims and provide financial payouts as per policy terms.

2. Brokers and Agents

Insurance brokers and agents act as intermediaries between property owners and insurance companies. They help clients select the most suitable insurance policies based on their specific requirements and provide guidance throughout the insurance process.

Role:

- Assess clients' insurance needs and recommend appropriate coverage.
- Facilitate the purchase of insurance policies.
- Assist clients with claims processing and policy management.

3. Regulatory Bodies

In India, the **Insurance Regulatory and Development Authority of India (IRDAI)** oversees the functioning of the insurance sector. IRDAI ensures that insurance policies are fair, transparent, and comply with legal standards, protecting the interests of policyholders.

Role:

- Regulate insurance companies and their practices.
- Ensure compliance with insurance laws and regulations.
- Protect policyholders' rights and promote fair insurance practices.

4. Reinsurers

Reinsurance companies provide backup coverage to primary insurers, allowing them to manage large claims and mitigate risks more effectively. Reinsurers play a vital role in maintaining the financial stability of insurance companies.

Role:

- Offer reinsurance policies to insurance companies.
- Help insurers manage and distribute risk.
- Provide financial support during large-scale claims events.

Regulatory Framework Governing Real Estate Insurance

The real estate insurance sector is governed by various regulations and guidelines to protect policyholders and ensure fair practices. In India, the regulatory framework is designed to maintain the integrity and reliability of insurance services, ensuring that property owners receive adequate protection and that insurers operate transparently.

1. **Insurance Regulatory and Development Authority of India (IRDAI)**

   IRDAI is the primary regulatory body overseeing the insurance sector in India. It formulates policies, sets guidelines, and ensures that insurance companies adhere to legal and ethical standards.

   Key Responsibilities:

   - Regulate the functioning of insurance companies.
   - Approve new insurance products and policy terms.
   - Monitor compliance with insurance regulations.
   - Protect the interests of policyholders by ensuring fair practices.

2. **The Insurance Act, 1938**

   The Insurance Act of 1938 establishes the legal framework for the registration, operation, and regulation of insurance companies in India. It outlines the requirements for insurance contracts, solvency margins, and the conduct of insurers.

   Key Provisions:

   - Mandates the registration of insurance companies with IRDAI.
   - Defines the terms and conditions for insurance contracts.
   - Specifies the financial and operational standards insurers must maintain.

3. **Pradhan Mantri Fasal Bima Yojana (PMFBY)**

   Although primarily aimed at agricultural properties, PMFBY highlights the government's role in promoting insurance for disaster-prone properties. It underscores the importance of insurance in mitigating risks associated with natural calamities.

Key Features:

- Provides financial support to farmers in the event of crop failure.
- Encourages the adoption of insurance practices for properties exposed to natural disasters.
- Enhances the resilience of vulnerable sectors against climate-related risks.

4. **Real Estate (Regulation and Development) Act, 2016 (RERA)**

RERA enforces transparency and accountability in real estate transactions, often requiring independent valuation reports for new projects to ensure fair pricing. While RERA primarily focuses on the regulation of real estate development, it indirectly impacts insurance practices by promoting ethical standards and transparency.

Impact on Insurance:

- Encourages developers to secure adequate insurance coverage for projects.
- Mandates disclosure of insurance details to protect homebuyers.
- Enhances trust and credibility in the real estate market through regulated practices.

Ethical and Legal Obligations of Valuers

Real estate insurance is intertwined with valuation practices, and both fields uphold stringent ethical and legal standards to ensure fairness and reliability. Valuers, who assess property values, must adhere to these principles to maintain the integrity of the real estate market.

1. **Impartiality and Objectivity**

   Valuers must remain impartial and objective in their assessments, avoiding conflicts of interest that could bias their evaluations. This ensures that valuations are fair and reliable, fostering trust among stakeholders.

2. **Confidentiality**

   Valuers are often privy to sensitive information about properties and clients. They must handle this data securely, ensuring it is only shared with authorized individuals or entities.

3. **Legal Compliance**

   Valuers must comply with all relevant local laws and regulations, including zoning laws, building codes, and taxation statutes. This ensures that valuations reflect the legal status and permissible uses of properties.

4. **Accountability**

   Valuers are accountable for the accuracy and fairness of their assessments. Inaccurate or biased valuations can lead to significant financial losses for stakeholders and legal consequences for the valuer.

Importance of Real Estate Insurance

Real estate insurance is indispensable for various stakeholders in the real estate market, providing multiple benefits that contribute to the overall stability and growth of the sector.

1. **Risk Mitigation**

   Real estate projects and property ownership are inherently associated with numerous risks, including natural disasters, accidents, theft, and legal disputes. Insurance acts as a safety net, protecting property owners and developers from substantial financial losses caused by these unforeseen events.

2. **Financial Security**

   Insurance provides financial security to property owners, investors, and developers by ensuring that they can recover from unexpected losses without facing severe financial strain. This security is crucial for maintaining the financial health and viability of real estate projects.

3. **Regulatory Compliance**

   In many cases, insurance is a mandatory requirement for securing loans, complying with legal obligations, and participating in certain real estate transactions. Compliance with insurance regulations ensures that developers and homebuyers meet legal standards and avoid penalties.

4. **Market Credibility**

   Proper insurance coverage enhances the credibility of stakeholders in the real estate market. Developers with comprehensive insurance plans are perceived as reliable and responsible, attracting more investors and buyers. Similarly, insured properties are more attractive to lenders and tenants, fostering trust and confidence in the market.

5. **Facilitating Smooth Transactions**

   Insurance plays a pivotal role in ensuring smooth real estate transactions by assuring all parties involved. It reduces uncertainties and financial risks, making property deals more secure and attractive.

The Role of Real Estate Insurance in Sustainable Development

As the real estate sector increasingly focuses on sustainability and eco-friendly practices, insurance is pivotal in supporting these initiatives. Sustainable real estate projects often require specialized insurance coverage to address unique risks and enhance their market appeal.

1. **Green Building Insurance**

   Green building insurance covers properties that incorporate sustainable and energy-efficient features. These buildings may have specialized construction materials, renewable energy systems, and advanced environmental technologies.

   Coverage Includes:

   - Protection for renewable energy installations like solar panels and wind turbines.
   - Coverage for sustainable construction materials and green technologies.
   - Liability coverage for environmental risks and compliance issues.

   Benefits:

   - Encourages the adoption of sustainable building practices.

- Provides financial protection for investments in green technologies.
- Enhances the market value and appeal of eco-friendly properties.

2. **Environmental Liability Insurance**

   Environmental liability insurance protects property owners and developers from financial losses arising from environmental damage caused by their properties. This is particularly relevant for properties located in environmentally sensitive areas or those involved in industrial activities.

   Coverage Includes:

   - Cleanup costs for environmental contamination.
   - Legal fees and settlements related to environmental lawsuits.
   - Compensation for third-party environmental damage claims.

   Benefits:

   - Mitigates the financial impact of environmental incidents.
   - Ensures compliance with environmental regulations.
   - Protects the reputation and sustainability credentials of property owners and developers.

3. **Incentives for Sustainable Real Estate Insurance**

   Insurance companies are increasingly offering incentives for properties that adhere to sustainable practices, such as reduced premiums for energy-efficient buildings or discounts for obtaining green certifications.

Incentives Include:

- Lower premiums for properties with certified green features.
- Rebates for implementing energy-efficient systems.
- Enhanced coverage options for sustainable developments.

Benefits:

- Reduces the cost of insurance for sustainable properties.
- Encourages investment in eco-friendly building practices.
- Aligns insurance products with global sustainability goals.

By integrating robust insurance strategies into their operations, developers and homebuyers alike can navigate the complexities of the real estate landscape with confidence, ensuring that their investments are well-protected and resilient against potential adversities.

Part 5

FINANCE FOR DEVELOPERS IN INDIA

Chapter 1

Overview of Developer Finance

Developer financing is a real estate development process, providing the necessary capital for developers to bring their projects from concept to reality. The nature of real estate development makes financing particularly complex, as it involves large-scale investments across multiple phases of a project, from land acquisition and construction to final sales or leasing. These projects can range from residential complexes to commercial developments, and the financial requirements vary significantly depending on the scale, scope, and timeline of the project. For instance, small residential projects may require less capital upfront compared to large mixed-use developments that combine residential, retail, and office spaces. Developers must navigate numerous challenges in securing the required funds, such as managing cash flow to ensure smooth operations, adhering to project timelines, and responding to fluctuations in market conditions. Real estate markets are highly sensitive to external factors, including interest rates, regulatory changes, and economic cycles, all of which can impact the availability of funding or the financial stability of a project. Therefore, developers need to be well-versed in the diverse financing options available, understanding the risks and benefits of each, to secure the necessary capital and successfully deliver their projects. By selecting the appropriate financing mix and understanding the dynamics of the market and their specific project needs, developers can mitigate financial challenges and ensure the successful execution of their real estate ventures.

Brief history of developers

The Real Estate and construction business inherently requires the investment of capital on a large scale. In Tier-I cities such as Delhi and Mumbai, this is magnified on account of the scarcity and high cost of land. All operations related to the field of the Real Estate business such as purchase of land, payment of premium on land, duties to be paid to the statutory bodies, cost of construction, rehabilitation of old occupants etc. Require heavy capital investment. All these expenses are incurred way before the completion of the sale units.

Developer Financing Needs

Real estate development involves significant capital outlay at different stages of the project lifecycle, including land acquisition, construction, and marketing. Developers require financing for:

- **Land Acquisition**: Developers need funds to acquire land or property for development. This can be the first significant financial hurdle in a project.
- **Construction Costs**: The bulk of financing needs arises during the construction phase, where funds are needed for materials, labor, permits, and infrastructure development.

- **Cash Flow Management**: Throughout the development process, maintaining cash flow is vital for smooth operations. Developers often require short-term financing to bridge gaps between expenses and income, especially in long-term projects.
- **Market Conditions**: Market fluctuations, regulatory changes, or delays can create financial challenges, requiring quick access to funding to maintain momentum and meet deadlines.
- **Exit Strategy**: Depending on the project type, developers may also require financing for the final stages, such as marketing, leasing, or selling units. Financing options may vary for short-term hold and long-term retention strategies.

Traditional Funding Avenues and Regulation of Funds under RERA

Before the enactment of the Real Estate (Regulation and Development) Act, 2016 (RERA), real estate developers in India often relied on informal and largely unregulated methods to raise capital for their projects. One common approach involved securing funds from private investors who made advance payments for units in upcoming developments, often at significantly discounted prices compared to market rates. In return, these investors were promised allocations of multiple units, sometimes with preferential rates. Additionally, developers frequently used pre-launch schemes, such as the 20:80 model, wherein consumers paid 20% of the total cost at booking and the remaining 80% at possession. These schemes generated early-stage funds, allowing developers to start construction and establish financial stability for the initial phases of the project.

However, these practices also had substantial risks. Developers often accepted bookings and advanced payments without securing necessary regulatory approvals or sanctioned plans for their projects. In some cases, units were sold before obtaining compliance certificates, leaving consumers vulnerable to project delays or abandonment. Frequent delays and unethical practices by some developers led to a significant erosion of consumer trust, particularly in pre-construction or under-construction projects. The lack of transparency, poor project management, and inadequate oversight created an environment of uncertainty, leaving many buyers in limbo as projects failed to meet promised timelines.

The introduction of RERA in 2016 significantly altered the funding dynamics for real estate developers. One of the key provisions of RERA mandates that developers deposit 70% of the proceeds from project sales into a separate escrow account, which can only be used for the specific project. This ensures that the funds are utilized solely for their intended purpose, protecting homebuyers and ensuring the completion of projects. While this regulation enhances consumer protection, it also impacts the short-term liquidity of developers, who are now unable to use these funds for other operational expenses.

Additionally, RERA prohibits developers from selling units without prior registration with the regulatory authority. This requires developers to meet various compliance standards, including securing necessary approvals and sanctioned plans before they can launch a project. As a result, developers are now restricted from raising initial capital through pre-sales of units, as was common before RERA, and must turn to alternative financing options such as debt or equity financing. This shift to more formal and regulated funding sources has forced developers to seek loans from banks, non-banking financial institutions (NBFCs), or through external commercial borrowings.

While the stricter regulations have created challenges for developers in securing initial capital, they have also led to several positive outcomes. Consumer confidence has increased, as funds are now more likely to be used for the completion of projects. Financial institutions, too, are more inclined to lend to developers, given the increased oversight and accountability under RERA. This has led to more responsible lending practices, creating new opportunities for project financing in the Indian real estate sector.

As developers adapt to these regulatory changes, many are turning to real estate project loans, which are available for both residential and commercial developments. These loans help maintain project construction timelines and ensure the timely delivery of projects. With flexible repayment terms, they provide developers with the necessary capital to bridge gaps created by RERA's funding restrictions.

In conclusion, while RERA has brought much-needed reforms to the Indian real estate sector—ensuring greater transparency and accountability—it has also reshaped the way developers raise and manage funds. As the industry adjusts to these changes, the evolution of financing options, along with stringent compliance requirements, is reshaping the landscape of real estate financing in India.

Chapter 2

Debt Financing for Developers

Debt financing represents a cornerstone in the financial strategies of developers in India, enabling them to secure requisite capital for diverse projects. This mechanism involves borrowing funds that are repaid over a prearranged tenure with interest, offering developers a viable avenue to address costs associated with operations, construction, land acquisition, or infrastructure without compromising equity stakes. The structured nature of debt financing ensures that developers can maintain control over their projects while aligning repayment schedules with anticipated revenue streams. Below is a comprehensive analysis of critical debt financing instruments tailored to the specificities of the Indian real estate development sector:

1. Bank Loans

Bank loans constitute a fundamental and traditional debt financing instrument for Indian developers, addressing a wide array of financial needs such as working capital, procurement of assets, or funding large-scale construction undertakings.

These loans are predominantly classified as secured, necessitating collateral such as land, ongoing projects, or completed assets, although unsecured variants are accessible based on the borrower's credit profile. The customization of bank loans in India permits tenures ranging from short-term arrangements to extended repayment schedules, affording developers operational flexibility. Interest rates are dynamically influenced by macroeconomic conditions, the financial solvency of the borrower, and the maturity of the loan. Additionally, banks often require a detailed project feasibility analysis and a robust repayment plan to mitigate their risk exposure.

Despite their liquidity advantages, the rigid repayment obligations linked to bank loans can present significant challenges if project revenues experience delays, underscoring the need for meticulous cash flow management and contingency planning to avert potential financial distress. In recent years, developers have also leveraged consortium loans, wherein multiple banks collaborate to finance large-scale projects, spreading risk and ensuring adequate capital availability.

Types of loans developers can apply for include term loans for capital expenditures, project loans for real estate development, and working capital loans for daily operations. Syndicated loans are another option for larger-scale projects. Interest rates typically range from 8% to 14% per annum, influenced by creditworthiness and economic context. RERA mandates developers disclose project financing details to ensure transparency, and banks may require compliance certificates under RERA for project approvals.

2. Non-Convertible Debentures (NCDs)

Non-Convertible Debentures (NCDs) serve as a pivotal funding instrument for developers seeking medium- to long-term capital without equity dilution. NCDs are structured as fixed-income instruments that cannot transition into equity, thus appealing to investors prioritizing stable returns. These debentures may be secured by underlying assets or unsecured, contingent upon the creditworthiness of the issuing entity. Developers leveraging NCDs benefit from higher capital infusion opportunities, albeit at relatively elevated interest rates compared to conventional bank loans. The issuance of NCDs is tightly regulated by the Securities and Exchange Board of India (SEBI) and is subject to credit agency ratings, which influence investor confidence and risk perception.

By providing a mechanism to mobilize substantial domestic capital, NCDs remain a critical financing alternative in the Indian real estate ecosystem. Furthermore, developers often structure NCDs to offer regular interest payouts, enhancing their attractiveness to institutional and retail investors. However, developers must navigate stringent disclosure norms and ensure timely servicing of interest obligations to maintain market credibility. The strategic use of NCDs has enabled many developers to fund large-scale residential and commercial projects, bridging the gap between demand for resources and available traditional financing options.

Types of NCDs include secured and unsecured variants, as well as fixed-rate and floating-rate instruments. Interest rates generally range from 9% to 12%, higher for unsecured NCDs. Eligibility often requires strong credit ratings and adherence to SEBI regulations. RERA ensures that NCD-funded projects maintain compliance with transparency and timelines, instilling trust in investors.

3. External Commercial Borrowings (ECBs)

External Commercial Borrowings (ECBs) facilitate access to international capital markets, enabling Indian developers to secure foreign currency loans at competitive interest rates. These instruments, governed by the Reserve Bank of India (RBI), are particularly advantageous for funding large-scale, capital-intensive endeavors such as infrastructure, commercial real estate, and industrial developments. ECBs typically offer cost efficiencies compared to domestic borrowing options; however, they expose developers to foreign exchange risks due to currency fluctuations, necessitating sophisticated hedging strategies to mitigate potential losses.

Regulatory stipulations impose restrictions on the end-use of ECBs, excluding speculative real estate transactions, thus ensuring alignment with developmental priorities. Additionally, developers must comply with intricate approval processes and adhere to borrowing caps stipulated by the RBI to ensure financial discipline. Despite these complexities, ECBs expand the financing horizon for Indian developers, integrating global capital into local markets. Many developers also leverage ECBs to access innovative financial products, such as green bonds, which align with sustainable development goals and offer favorable terms for environmentally conscious projects. By diversifying their funding sources through ECBs, developers can achieve a competitive edge while enhancing project viability.

Types of ECBs include direct loans, bonds (e.g., green bonds), and supplier credits for importing capital goods. Interest rates often range between 4% and 8%. Eligibility depends on RBI's ECB framework, with compliance required for borrowing caps and end-use restrictions. RERA ensures that ECB-funded projects are transparent, with reports on fund utilization and adherence to approved timelines.

4. Bridge Loans

Bridge loans, a short-term financing modality, address the immediate liquidity exigencies of developers during transitional phases of project execution. These loans are instrumental in bridging funding gaps preceding the arrangement of long-term financing or monetization of assets. Typically secured by collateral such as receivables, unsold inventory, or under-construction assets, bridge loans carry elevated interest rates reflective of their short tenures and urgency. Developers deploy bridge loans strategically to mitigate cash flow mismatches, with repayment often synchronized with anticipated inflows from project completions or asset disposals.

While bridge loans are a critical instrument for maintaining operational continuity, their high cost necessitates prudent usage to avert financial overextension. Additionally, developers must ensure that the anticipated revenue streams or alternative financing arrangements materialize within the stipulated timeframes to avoid default risks. In the context of the Indian real estate market, bridge loans have emerged as a lifeline for developers navigating regulatory changes, market volatility, or unforeseen delays in project approvals. By offering immediate liquidity, these loans enable developers to sustain project momentum, ensuring timely delivery and maintaining stakeholder confidence.

Types of bridge loans include secured loans backed by collateral and unsecured loans with higher interest rates. Interest rates typically range from 12% to 20%. Eligibility often requires proof of future inflows and collateral security. Under RERA, developers must provide fund utilization details and ensure loans are applied solely to registered projects.

5. NBFC's

India's financial sector has long been dominated by traditional banks. However, Non-Banking Financial Companies (NBFCs) have emerged as significant players, particularly in financing unorganized markets. From their inception, NBFCs have focused on infrastructure financing and have successfully carved out a competitive niche by offering medium-term funding with greater flexibility than banks. This advantage has made them an attractive alternative for real estate developers and other borrowers.

NBFCs are distinguished by their ability to make quicker decisions, assume higher risks, and customize their offerings to meet client-specific demands. Additional benefits include a diverse range of financial products, lower costs, wider market reach, robust risk management capabilities, and a deep understanding of their target customer groups. Despite these strengths, the growing composite demand within sectors like real estate often outpaces the available funding, leaving financing gaps that NBFCs strive to fill.

Role of NBFCs in Real Estate Financing

The real estate and construction sectors rely on unique financing structures, sourcing funds from state governments, banks, NBFCs, home finance companies, microfinance institutions, private capital, and individual investors. Among these, NBFCs have played a transformative role. Unlike banks, NBFCs are allowed to accept foreign funds via external commercial borrowings (ECB), as per Reserve Bank of India (RBI) regulations, enabling them to route these funds to infrastructure projects. However, they are prohibited from funding land acquisition directly. To navigate this restriction, NBFCs often provide financing for ongoing projects, giving developers liquidity that can indirectly facilitate land purchases.

How NBFCs Differ from Traditional Banks and Their Role in Real Estate Financing

Non-Banking Financial Companies (NBFCs) share similarities with traditional banks in terms of lending and investment but have distinct differences that make them a complementary financing option rather than a substitute:

Inability to Accept Demand Deposits: Unlike banks, NBFCs cannot accept funds that are repayable on demand, which are a primary source of liquidity for banks.

Limited Role in the Payment System: NBFCs are not part of the payment and settlement system and cannot issue checks drawn on themselves.

No Deposit Insurance: While banks provide deposit insurance through the Deposit Insurance and Credit Guarantee Corporation, NBFCs do not offer such coverage for their depositors.

These differences highlight the unique operational model of NBFCs. However, their flexibility and speed in addressing funding needs make them crucial players, especially in sectors like real estate. For instance:

Flexibility in Loan Structuring: NBFCs offer customizable loan terms, allowing developers to structure repayment schedules that align with cash flow expectations, which is beneficial for projects with staggered or uncertain revenue generation.

Support for Redevelopment Projects: NBFCs are vital in financing redevelopment initiatives, including self-redevelopment projects or ventures that have stalled due to lack of liquidity. Their quicker decision-making processes enable them to provide timely funding to such projects.

Faster Approval Processes: The streamlined approval process of NBFCs is particularly advantageous for cash-strapped developers in the affordable housing sector, where urgent funding is often necessary to keep projects moving forward.

Advantages of NBFCs for Real Estate Developers

Faster Loan Approvals: NBFCs expedite the loan application and approval process, critical for time-sensitive projects.

Simpler Processes: Borrowers benefit from streamlined procedures with fewer bureaucratic hurdles.

No Minimum Deposit Requirement: This makes NBFCs more accessible for developers with limited upfront capital.

Focus on Affordable Housing: Government initiatives to promote affordable housing, especially in semi-urban and rural areas, have further encouraged developers to engage with NBFCs. Incentives and infrastructural status for affordable housing projects make them a promising sector for NBFC financing.

Government Regulations and Their Impact

The RBI's decision to allow NBFCs to access foreign funds through ECBs has broadened their capacity to fund infrastructure projects, boosting the real estate market.

Recent regulatory changes emphasize transparency, requiring NBFCs to comply with strict fund utilization norms and reporting mechanisms.

While NBFCs are restricted from funding land acquisitions, their ability to channel funds into ongoing projects indirectly supports land purchase requirements.

These regulatory frameworks ensure that NBFCs operate within defined boundaries while fostering innovation and growth in the real estate financing landscape.

Challenges and Opportunities for NBFCs

Despite their benefits, NBFCs operate in a challenging environment. The Indian banking sector's cautious approach to real estate lending, driven by rising non-performing assets (NPAs), has created an opportunity for NBFCs to supply affordable funds, particularly in low-risk segments. However, NBFCs must maintain robust risk management practices to control bad debts and ensure sustainable growth.

The sector also faces regulatory oversight from the RBI, which governs their operations, sets borrowing limits, and imposes restrictions on end-use funds. Nevertheless, NBFCs have leveraged these challenges to refine their offerings, tapping into domestic and foreign capital markets to provide customized solutions.

The Growing Importance of NBFC Financing

Private equity funds, commercial banks, and NBFCs together form the backbone of India's real estate financing ecosystem. While bank lending to real estate has been on a decline, NBFC financing has grown steadily, driven by their ability to cater to underserved segments of the market. With their mature capabilities, NBFCs are positioned to meet the increasing demand for flexible financing options while maintaining strong returns for their stakeholders.

Chapter 3

Equity Financing for Developers

1. Private Equity

Private equity represents capital raised from private sources, such as business owners, partners, or shareholders. It is often referred to as self-investment since the funds come directly from individuals or entities that have a stake in the business. In real estate projects, private equity is a crucial part of financing, as it provides the necessary capital to secure land, develop properties, or expand operations.

Key Characteristics of Private Equity:

Ownership and Control: Investors in private equity typically gain a share in the ownership of the project or business, which may come with rights to influence decisions. This is especially true for external investors who look to capitalize on the growth of the business.

Capital Deployment: Private equity is often used to meet significant capital requirements, especially in the early or development stages of a project, such as acquiring real estate or building infrastructure.

Returns: Investors usually expect returns through dividends, appreciation in share value, or a profit share based on the project's overall success.

Risk Profile: Private equity is considered a higher-risk investment because the funds invested are illiquid. Investors may not see returns immediately, and in some cases, the investment may not yield positive results if the business or project does not perform as expected.

2. Preferred Equity

Preferred equity is a type of equity investment in which investors receive priority in terms of income distributions and liquidation proceeds compared to common equity holders. This form of equity is a hybrid between debt and equity and is often used in India to balance risk and reward for investors who seek a more secure return but are still willing to participate in a project's potential success. It has gained popularity in India due to its flexibility and ability to address financing gaps in the real estate sector.

Key Features of Preferred Equity in India

Equity, Not Debt: Preferred equity is categorized as equity rather than debt, meaning it does not require regular debt service payments. Instead, distributions are contingent on the availability of cash flow. Cash flows are distributed after covering senior loan obligations, operational expenses, and any reserve requirements. This arrangement provides developers (sponsors) in India with flexibility during periods of financial uncertainty or project delays, which are common due to regulatory and approval challenges in the Indian real estate market.

Customized Terms: Preferred equity agreements in India are highly flexible and tailored to the specific needs of each transaction. Unlike standardised loan documents, developers and investors can negotiate terms that align with the project's financial and operational requirements. These agreements often incorporate innovative structures, such as multi-tiered waterfalls or equity kickers, to balance risks and returns effectively. In India, this flexibility is particularly useful in navigating varying project timelines and regulatory requirements under laws like the Real Estate (Regulation and Development) Act, 2016 (RERA).

Priority in Distributions: Preferred equity holders enjoy a higher priority in the capital stack than common equity holders. This ensures they receive distributions before common equity holders, reducing their risk exposure. If a project underperforms, losses are absorbed by the common equity holders—typically the developers—before impacting preferred equity investors. In India, this is particularly advantageous given the market volatility in cities like Mumbai, Bengaluru, and Delhi NCR.

Advantages for Investors in India

Risk Mitigation: Preferred equity is safer in the capital stack than common equity. This means that in cases of financial underperformance—due to factors like regulatory delays, market fluctuations, or oversupply—investors in preferred equity are more likely to recoup their investments.

Attractive Returns: Preferred equity in India offers higher returns compared to senior debt while maintaining a lower risk profile than common equity. This balance makes it an appealing choice for investors seeking steady and higher-yielding income, especially in high-demand sectors such as residential housing, office spaces, and mixed-use developments.

Investment Expertise: Investors in preferred equity often bring significant real estate experience. In India, this expertise is crucial for navigating complex regulatory environments, tax structures, and market dynamics, ensuring high-quality due diligence and better decision-making.

Benefits for Developers (Sponsors)

Increased Leverage: Preferred equity enables developers to increase project leverage by filling the gap between senior debt and common equity. This is particularly useful in India, where financing gaps often arise due to limited availability of traditional loans and strict lending norms imposed by banks and non-banking financial companies (NBFCs).

Preservation of Control: Developers retain operational control over the project, as preferred equity investors typically do not engage in the day-to-day management. This allows Indian sponsors to focus on executing their vision while leveraging external funds to complete ambitious projects.

Promote and Profit Sharing: Indian developers often receive a "promote" or a share of the profits, typically around 30%, as compensation for their expertise and efforts in managing the project. This is in addition to returns on their equity contributions, making it a lucrative option for sponsors with high-growth projects.

Use Cases for Preferred Equity in India

- **Development Projects**: Preferred equity is frequently used to fund ground-up developments in cities like Mumbai, Bengaluru, and Pune, covering costs such as land acquisition, zoning, and construction.
- **Property Acquisitions**: It facilitates the purchase of profitable properties or distressed assets, providing developers the flexibility to seize opportunities without relying solely on debt financing.
- **Rescue Financing**: Developers can use preferred equity as a lifeline for projects facing operational deficits or financial distress. This includes covering costs during market downturns or negotiating favourable loan terms with banks or NBFCs.
- **Capital Restructuring**: Preferred equity is a tool for monetizing a sponsor's existing equity, enabling them to buy out partners, meet regulatory capital requirements, or avoid prepayment penalties associated with refinancing senior debt.

Structure of Preferred Equity Investments in India

Placement in the Capital Stack

Preferred equity sits between senior debt and common equity in the capital stack. This position provides it with a priority claim on cash flows and distributions, which is vital in India's market, where senior lenders often impose strict repayment schedules.

Distribution of Cash Flow

Preferred equity investors in India typically receive:

First, the cumulative preferred return (often 10% annually).

Second, the return of their initial capital investment.

Finally, a share of residual profits, distributed according to the agreed-upon terms.

Waterfall Distribution

In a typical waterfall structure, proceeds from project operations or sale are allocated in tiers, ensuring preferred equity investors are compensated before common equity holders. This aligns with the risk appetite of investors looking for predictable returns in the Indian market.

Additional Features of Preferred Equity in India

Non-Recourse Nature

Preferred equity investments in India are generally non-recourse, meaning investors are not personally liable for the project's obligations. Exceptions may include standard carve-outs for fraud, mismanagement, or non-compliance with RERA guidelines.

No Capital Calls

Preferred equity investors are protected from future capital calls, as the responsibility for additional funding falls on the sponsor. This feature is crucial in India, where cost overruns or regulatory delays are common.

Flexible Exit Strategies

Preferred equity in India can be structured with multiple exit options, such as conversion into common equity, sale of the project, or co-GP (co-general partner) arrangements. These strategies provide flexibility to adapt to changing market conditions and investor preferences.

3. Common Equity

Common equity represents the ownership stake in a business or real estate project that is subject to the greatest risk but also offers the highest potential for return. Common equity investors are last in line to receive payments, which makes their investment riskier. However, they stand to benefit the most if the project succeeds, as they share in the profits generated by the business or project.

Key Features of Common Equity

Ownership and Decision-Making: In India, common equity holders have ownership rights in the real estate project. These rights often include decision-making power regarding major aspects of the project, such as design, financing strategies, and exit plans. For sponsors (developers), common equity reflects their skin in the game and demonstrates commitment to the project.

Risk and Reward Dynamics: Common equity occupies the lowest position in the capital stack, making it the most exposed to project risks. However, it also provides the potential for high returns if the project performs well. In India, the real estate sector's growth in metropolitan areas and rising property values make common equity attractive despite its risks.

No Fixed Returns: Unlike debt or preferred equity, common equity does not guarantee fixed returns. Investors share in the residual profits after operational costs, senior debt obligations, and preferred equity distributions. This aligns their interests with the long-term success of the project.

Market-Specific Features

- In India, common equity is often tied to **joint development agreements (JDAs)** or **special purpose vehicles (SPVs)**, where developers and landowners/investors partner for project execution.

- It is common for sponsors to provide the land as equity in the project, while investors contribute capital.

Advantages of Common Equity in India

High Return Potential: The booming Indian real estate market, particularly in metropolitan and tier-2 cities, offers significant appreciation potential. Common equity holders benefit directly from this upside.

Alignment with Market Growth: With rapid urbanization and infrastructure development, common equity allows investors to capitalize on long-term growth trends in Indian real estate.

Flexibility in Project Structuring: real estate projects often use common equity to attract additional funding. Sponsors can showcase their commitment by holding a substantial equity stake, and building confidence among other investors.

Ownership and Control: Common equity holders (often sponsors) maintain operational control of the project, ensuring that their vision is executed while retaining decision-making power over key aspects such as project timelines and marketing strategies.

Challenges of Common Equity

High Risk Exposure: Common equity is the first to absorb losses if a project underperforms. In India, market fluctuations, regulatory changes, and approval delays can significantly impact project viability.

Dependence on External Factors: Common equity returns depend on the project's success, which is influenced by factors like economic conditions, demand-supply dynamics, and changes in policies such as the Goods and Services Tax (GST) or Real Estate (Regulation and Development) Act, 2016 (RERA).

Regulatory Complexity: Indian real estate projects involve multiple layers of approvals and compliance, increasing the timeline and risk for common equity holders. Projects under RERA require strict adherence to timelines and disclosures, which can impact equity returns.

Applications of Common Equity

Residential and Commercial Projects: Common equity is widely used in residential and commercial developments, especially in urban centres like Mumbai, Delhi NCR, Bengaluru, and Hyderabad, where demand for housing and office spaces is robust.

Joint Development Agreements (JDAs): In India, JDAs are a popular method of structuring common equity investments. Landowners contribute their land as equity, while developers invest capital and expertise. Profits are shared based on the agreed-upon terms.

Special Purpose Vehicles (SPVs): Many large-scale projects in India are executed through SPVs, where investors pool funds in the form of common equity. This structure isolates the project's financial risks from the parent company's balance sheet.

Redevelopment Projects: Common equity plays a significant role in redevelopment initiatives, such as transforming old housing societies in cities like Mumbai into modern residential complexes. Sponsors often contribute equity to gain a stake in the project's future profits.

Structure of Common Equity in India

Placement in the Capital Stack

Common equity sits at the bottom of the capital stack, below senior debt and preferred equity. It has the highest risk but also the highest potential reward.

Profit Distribution

Residual profits from operations or sales are distributed to common equity holders after fulfilling all other financial obligations, such as debt repayment and preferred equity distributions.

Use in Financing

Common equity is often used to secure additional funding, such as construction finance or preferred equity, by demonstrating the sponsor's commitment to the project.

Comparison: Common Equity vs. Preferred Equity in India

Aspect	Common Equity	Preferred Equity
Risk	Highest, absorbs first losses	Moderate, prioritized over common equity
Returns	Residual, potentially unlimited	Fixed, cumulative returns
Position in Stack	Lowest, last to receive distributions	Higher, receives distributions before common equity
Control	Full voting and management rights	Typically passive, no operational control

Aspect	Common Equity	Preferred Equity
Role in Project	Ownership and decision-making	Financial support with reduced risk exposure

4. Crowd-Funding

Crowd-funding has become an increasingly popular method of raising capital in India, particularly in the real estate sector, where it offers an innovative alternative to traditional financing options. It allows businesses and startups to access funding from a wide range of small investors, typically through online platforms, enabling broader participation in investment opportunities.

Key Features of Crowd-Funding in India:

Access to Capital from a Large Pool of Investors: Crowd-funding provides real estate developers and small businesses in India with an opportunity to raise funds from a large number of individual investors, rather than relying on banks or private equity. This can be particularly advantageous for businesses or developers who may face challenges securing financing through conventional channels.

Online Platforms as Intermediaries: The process is facilitated through specialized online platforms such as **Ketto**, **Wishberry**, **Explara**, and international platforms like **Fundrise**, which cater to Indian investors. These platforms act as intermediaries, connecting project sponsors with a wide pool of investors. Investors can browse various investment opportunities and choose projects that align with their interests or financial goals.

1. **Lower Investment Thresholds:** One of the main attractions of crowd-funding in India is its ability to allow individuals to

invest with relatively small amounts. Traditionally, real estate investment required significant capital, but with crowd-funding, investors can contribute as little as INR 5,000-10,000, making it accessible to a broader demographic, including millennials, middle-class families, and small retail investors.

2. **Investment in Specific Projects:** Crowd-funding for real estate in India often allows investors to participate in specific property projects or developments. These could include residential, commercial, or mixed-use developments. Investors typically have access to detailed project information, such as estimated returns, risks, timelines, and market analysis. This transparency helps them make more informed investment decisions.

3. **Risk and Return:** While crowd-funding in real estate presents the potential for significant returns, it also carries risks. Real estate projects in India can face delays, regulatory hurdles, cost overruns, or market volatility. Platforms generally provide risk assessments, but like any investment, there is no guarantee of returns. It's important for investors to conduct thorough due diligence before committing capital to a project.

Benefits of Crowd-Funding in India:

1. **Diversification for Investors:** Crowd-funding platforms in India offer a wide variety of projects, allowing investors to diversify their portfolios across multiple real estate developments. This reduces the risk associated with putting all funds into a single investment and helps investors spread their exposure across different types of properties or geographical areas.

2. **Democratization of Investment:** In the past, large-scale real estate investments in India were mainly accessible to high-net-worth individuals (HNWIs) or institutional investors.

Crowd-funding democratizes this by allowing people with modest savings to participate in the market. This shifts the focus toward a more inclusive investment model, where everyone has the opportunity to invest, regardless of income level.

3. **Faster Capital Mobilization:** Traditional financing channels such as bank loans or private equity can take months or even years to secure. In contrast, crowd-funding allows real estate developers to raise capital quickly and efficiently, often within weeks. This faster access to funding enables developers to initiate projects sooner, benefiting both the developers and the investors.

4. **Regulatory Support and Growth Potential:** India's regulatory environment has also evolved to support crowd-funding platforms. The Securities and Exchange Board of India (SEBI) is gradually developing guidelines for alternative investment platforms, and the government is increasingly supportive of fintech innovations. This regulatory backing is expected to encourage the growth of crowd-funding in India, making it a more secure and attractive option for both investors and developers.

Challenges in the Indian Market:

Despite its potential, crowd-funding for real estate in India faces several challenges:

- **Regulatory and Legal Framework:** The lack of a comprehensive regulatory framework around crowd-funding in India remains a concern. While SEBI is working on guidelines, regulatory uncertainty could deter some investors.

- **Market Trust:** Since crowd-funding for real estate is still relatively new in India, some investors may be sceptical about the legitimacy of platforms or the viability of projects.
- **Economic Volatility:** The real estate sector in India is subject to fluctuations based on factors such as interest rates, market sentiment, and government policy. This can affect the performance of crowd-funded projects.

Examples of crowdfunding in India

(i) The Avenues (Mumbai)

- **Developer:** Lodha Group
- **Platform:** SmartCrowd

Why Crowdfunding: Lodha Group used SmartCrowd to raise capital for a premium residential project in Mumbai. They sought a large pool of small investors to diversify funding sources and speed up capital mobilization, bypassing the traditional and often time-consuming methods of obtaining bank loans or private equity.

(ii) Goregaon East (Mumbai)

- **Developer:** Indiabulls Real Estate
- **Platform:** SmartCrowd

Why Crowdfunding: Indiabulls turned to crowdfunding to access capital quickly for a residential project catering to the middle-income housing segment in Mumbai. By using crowdfunding, they were able to attract smaller investors and mitigate the reliance on traditional financing sources, thus streamlining the funding process.

(iii) Affordable Housing Project (Mumbai)

- **Developer:** Kailash Nath Group
- **Platform:** Ketto

Why Crowdfunding: Kailash Nath Group used Ketto to fund an affordable housing project in Mumbai, catering to middle-class families. The developer sought capital quickly, and crowdfunding allowed them to access a wider base of small investors who wanted to contribute to affordable housing solutions.

(iv) Bengaluru Residential Development

- **Developer:** Prestige Group
- **Platform:** Fundrise

Why Crowdfunding: Prestige Group used Fundrise to raise funds for a residential development targeting professionals in Bengaluru's booming tech sector. The group used crowdfunding to attract a wide range of investors and raise capital quickly for a high-demand project.

Investors in these real estate crowdfunding projects typically received fractional ownership, allowing them to own a portion of specific properties. This model enabled them to share in both the appreciation of the property's value and the rental income it generated. As the property's market value increased over time, investors stood to benefit from capital gains. Additionally, investors received a share of the rental income generated by tenants leasing the units, providing them with a steady stream of passive income. This approach allowed smaller investors to participate in high-value real estate ventures with the potential for attractive returns.

5. Foreign Direct Investment (FDI)

Foreign Direct Investment (FDI) involves investments made by a foreign company or individual in a business or real estate project located in another country. FDI is a crucial source of capital for many developing countries, including India, and plays a significant role in the growth of the real estate sector. It typically involves obtaining a controlling interest or significant ownership stake in the business or project.

Key Features of Foreign Direct Investment:

Direct Control or Influence:

Unlike foreign portfolio investment, which involves buying stocks or bonds without seeking control, FDI generally entails obtaining a controlling or significant ownership interest. This means foreign investors not only provide capital but also often seek a level of influence or control over the operations of the business or project.

Long-Term Investment:

FDI is typically a long-term investment. Foreign investors are usually committed to staying in the business for a considerable period and are willing to deal with the risks associated with international investments, such as currency fluctuations, regulatory changes, and political instability.

Influence on the Local Economy:

FDI can have a significant impact on the local economy by introducing capital, expertise, and technology. It often leads to the creation of jobs, infrastructure development, and improved business practices in the local market.

Regulation and Control:

Most countries have specific regulations governing FDI, especially in sectors like real estate. In India, for example, the government allows FDI in real estate development but has set certain guidelines regarding the type of properties, landholding limits, and the timeline for project completion.

Risks and Challenges of FDI:

Political and Economic Risk:

Foreign investors are exposed to political and economic risks, such as changes in government policies, fluctuations in currency value, and regulatory shifts. These risks can affect the profitability and viability of real estate investments.

Legal and Regulatory Barriers:

Many countries impose strict regulations on FDI, especially in sensitive sectors like real estate. This can make it difficult for foreign investors to enter the market or may require navigating complex legal and bureaucratic processes.

Cultural and Operational Differences:

Investors from foreign countries may face challenges related to cultural differences, local market conditions, and operational hurdles. They may need to adapt to local customs, business practices, and regulations.

Examples of FDI's In India

(i) DLF Cyber City (Gurugram)

- **Developer:** DLF Limited
- **FDI Investor: Morgan Stanley** (via a joint venture)

DLF Cyber City is one of the most prominent commercial real estate developments in Gurugram, catering to the growing demand for office space from multinational corporations and tech companies. Morgan Stanley, a global investment firm, partnered with DLF to co-develop and invest in parts of this large-scale development. The project benefited from FDI through this strategic partnership, which provided substantial capital for its expansion.

(ii) Lodha Group - The World Towers (Mumbai)

- **Developer:** Lodha Group
- **FDI Investor: Goldman Sachs, JP Morgan** (via funding and partnerships)

The World Towers is a luxury residential project in Mumbai, comprising some of the tallest residential towers in India. The project received significant FDI from global investors, including financial giants such as Goldman Sachs and JP Morgan. These investors provided funding for the project's development, particularly for the construction of high-end residential spaces in one of Mumbai's prime locations.

(iii) Embassy TechVillage (Bengaluru)

- **Developer:** Embassy Group
- **FDI Investor: Blackstone Group**

Embassy TechVillage is a commercial office complex located in Bengaluru, catering to IT companies and multinational corporations. The development, which spans several acres, is home to major global companies. Blackstone, one of the world's largest private equity firms, invested in this tech park, providing FDI that helped to finance the development of world-class office spaces.

(iv) India Bulls One International (Mumbai)

- **Developer:** Indiabulls Real Estate
- **FDI Investor: The International Finance Corporation (IFC)**

Indiabulls One International is a high-end commercial real estate project in Mumbai, designed to offer office space for multinational corporations. The project received FDI from the International Finance Corporation (IFC), part of the World Bank, which helped finance the development of modern office infrastructure in Mumbai.

(v) Tata Housing - The Residence (Gurugram)

- **Developer:** Tata Housing Development Company
- **FDI Investor: Abu Dhabi Investment Authority (ADIA)**

The Residence is a luxury residential project by Tata Housing in Gurugram, designed to cater to high-net-worth individuals and expats. The project received FDI from the Abu Dhabi Investment Authority (ADIA), one of the world's largest sovereign wealth funds. The funds helped Tata Housing expand its portfolio of luxury residential projects in India.

(vi) Mahindra World City (Chennai)

- **Developer:** Mahindra Lifespace Developers
- **FDI Investor: Shenzhen-based China Development Bank (CDB)**

Mahindra World City is an integrated business city that includes residential, commercial, and industrial developments. The project received funding from China Development Bank (CDB) to help develop the infrastructure and attract international companies to establish manufacturing and office operations in the region.

FDI in real estate has played a crucial role in the development of some of India's most iconic and large-scale real estate projects. The involvement of global investors such as **Goldman Sachs**, **Blackstone**, and **Morgan Stanley** has enabled Indian developers to expand their project portfolios, bring international expertise, and improve infrastructure across residential, commercial, and industrial sectors. FDI has contributed significantly to the growth of cities like Mumbai, Gurugram, Bengaluru, and Chennai, transforming them into key global business hubs.

6. Foreign Institutional Investor (FII)

Foreign Institutional Investors (FII) are entities that pool capital from various investors to invest in assets such as stocks, bonds, or real estate projects across global markets. In India, FIIs have become significant contributors to the real estate sector, bringing capital, expertise, and strategic partnerships. Their role in the Indian real estate market has grown steadily over the years, as they seek opportunities in both residential and commercial real estate developments. FIIs primarily invest in publicly traded real estate companies, real estate investment trusts (REITs), and direct real estate ventures, thereby aiding in capital formation for the sector.

Key Features of Foreign Institutional Investors (FII) in Indian Real Estate

Portfolio Investment

Unlike Foreign Direct Investment (FDI), which typically involves direct ownership and control of real estate projects, FII investments are primarily portfolio investments in publicly listed real estate companies, funds, and REITs. FIIs do not seek control over the management of real estate companies but invest in them for returns generated through price appreciation and dividends.

Medium-Term Investment Horizon:

FIIs generally adopt a medium-term investment horizon when investing in Indian real estate. While they are focused on capitalizing on market trends, FIIs may hold their investments for several years, especially when the real estate market is poised for growth. They tend to invest in both residential and commercial sectors, including office spaces, malls, and industrial parks, with the aim of gaining returns from these assets' appreciation and rental yields.

Liquidity and Flexibility:

One of the key advantages of FII investments in Indian real estate is liquidity. Since FIIs invest through listed real estate companies or REITs, their investments are more liquid than traditional direct investments in properties. This liquidity allows FIIs to easily buy or sell securities in the stock market, making it easier for them to adjust their portfolios in response to market conditions.

Impact on the Indian Real Estate Market:

FIIs play a vital role in deepening India's capital markets and increasing liquidity, particularly in the real estate sector. Their investments in listed real estate companies or REITs enhance market efficiency, aid in price discovery, and provide much-needed capital to developers for project expansion. FIIs' large-scale investments in commercial real estate have helped fuel the growth of office spaces, retail developments, and infrastructure projects, further contributing to India's urbanization and economic growth.

Regulation and Control:

FIIs in India are regulated by the Securities and Exchange Board of India (SEBI), which sets guidelines on their investments in the real estate sector. These regulations include limits on the percentage of company shares that FIIs can own in a real estate company, as well as rules concerning disclosures and insider trading. SEBI ensures that FII investments comply with local laws, fostering a transparent and stable investment environment.

Risks and Challenges of FII Investments in Indian Real Estate

Market Volatility:

Like any other investment, FII investments in Indian real estate are subject to market volatility. Real estate markets can experience fluctuations due to changing demand, economic slowdowns, and shifts in government policies. FIIs may face challenges if the Indian real estate market faces price corrections, especially in a rapidly changing economic environment.

Currency and Political Risks:

FIIs investing in Indian real estate are exposed to foreign exchange risks, especially when the Indian Rupee depreciates against their home currencies. Additionally, political risks, such as changes in government policies or taxation laws, can impact the real estate market and alter the profitability of FII investments. Regulatory changes, such as new taxes or restrictions on property ownership, could also have an adverse effect on returns.

Global Economic Conditions:

Since FIIs operate globally, they are affected by international economic conditions. Global interest rates, inflation, and geopolitical events can impact their investment strategies in India. A downturn in major global economies can lead to reduced investment in India's real estate sector, thus affecting the overall demand and pricing in the market.

7. Family Office / High-Net-Worth Individuals (HNIs) in Real Estate

In the world of high-net-worth individuals (HNWIs) and ultra-high-net-worth individuals (UHNWIs), wealth management extends far beyond basic financial investments. At the heart of this sophisticated wealth structure are family offices, which provide a comprehensive suite of financial services designed to preserve and grow the wealth of affluent families over generations. Real estate investment plays a pivotal role in these strategies, not only for wealth generation but also for diversification, tax optimization, and legacy planning. In this detailed analysis, we delve into the intersection of family offices and real estate, exploring why this sector continues to thrive as an essential asset class for the wealthy.

What Is a Family Office in Real Estate?

A family office is a private wealth management advisory firm that serves ultra-high-net-worth individuals (UHNWIs) and affluent families. In the context of real estate, a family office manages the real estate investments of the family, ensuring these investments align with their broader financial goals. The real estate division within a family office is tasked with all activities related to property acquisitions, management, development, and disposals.

The primary mission of a family office in real estate is to help the family grow and protect its wealth through strategic real estate investments, often focusing on long-term holdings such as residential, commercial, and industrial properties. By leveraging the family's financial resources and expertise, these offices navigate the complexities of the real estate market and use this asset class to drive both wealth preservation and growth.

The Purpose of a Family Office

The overarching purpose of a family office is to manage the complete financial and non-financial aspects of a family's wealth. This includes not just managing investments but also ensuring tax optimization, estate planning, and philanthropy align with the family's values and long-term goals. A family office typically provides a holistic service package that covers:

Wealth Preservation: The office ensures that wealth is safeguarded over multiple generations, using a combination of investment strategies, estate planning, and tax optimization.

Investment Management: Strategic asset allocation, including both traditional and alternative investments like real estate.

Tax Optimization: Structuring the family's investments in ways that minimize tax liabilities, utilizing strategies like tax-efficient investment vehicles, capital gains deferral, and tax deductions from real estate.

Estate Planning: Ensuring the wealth is passed on to heirs in an efficient manner, often using trust structures to maintain privacy and minimize estate taxes.

Philanthropy: Family offices also play a role in managing charitable contributions and legacy-building activities through foundations and charitable trusts.

The core goal is to sustain and build wealth across generations, addressing both the financial and emotional needs of the family while ensuring that the wealth is used to benefit future generations.

Why Do Family Offices Invest in Real Estate?

Family offices are consistently drawn to real estate due to its multifaceted benefits that help meet their long-term financial goals. Real estate is often regarded as a stable and resilient asset class that can provide consistent returns and opportunities for wealth appreciation. Below are some of the primary reasons why family offices allocate significant portions of their portfolios to real estate:

Wealth Preservation: Real estate has proven to be one of the most stable asset classes, providing families with long-term security and protection against inflation and market volatility. Physical assets like land and buildings tend to hold their value, often appreciating over time.

Diversification: Investing in real estate helps family offices diversify their portfolios. Since real estate generally behaves differently from traditional assets like stocks and bonds, it offers a hedge against the volatility of the financial markets, reducing overall portfolio risk.

Income Generation: Many real estate assets, especially rental properties, generate a reliable stream of income through lease agreements. This cash flow provides families with liquidity that can be reinvested or used for other financial needs, making real estate an attractive option for those seeking consistent earnings.

Control and Flexibility: Family offices have significant control over their real estate investments. They can choose which properties to acquire, decide when to sell, and implement strategies to enhance property values through management, development, and redevelopment.

Tax Optimization: Real estate investments provide families with opportunities for tax savings. Depreciation, tax deductions, and tax-deferred exchanges (e.g., 1031 exchanges) allow family offices to minimize their tax liabilities.

Capital Appreciation: Over time, real estate properties tend to increase in value. This capital appreciation drives wealth accumulation and ensures that the family's real estate portfolio contributes to long-term financial growth.

Types of Real Estate Investments for Family Offices

The real estate investments made by family offices are highly diversified, often spanning across different sectors and property types. These investments may include:

Residential Properties: These range from high-end luxury estates to multi-family properties. Residential real estate offers a stable stream of rental income, with the added potential for capital appreciation over time. Family offices typically target prime residential locations that ensure long-term value retention.

Commercial Real Estate: This includes office buildings, retail centres, and industrial properties. These investments are typically long-term, as they generate rental income through lease agreements. Family offices may invest in established commercial properties or in development projects, such as mixed-use developments, to capitalize on urban growth.

Industrial Real Estate: With the rise of e-commerce, demand for warehouses, distribution centres, and industrial parks has surged. These properties offer high returns due to the increasing need for logistics spaces driven by online retail trends.

Real Estate Funds: Rather than directly purchasing physical properties, some family offices invest in private equity real estate funds. These funds pool capital from various investors and focus on a diversified portfolio of real estate assets, providing access to larger-scale investment opportunities.

Development Projects: Family offices also invest in real estate development and redevelopment projects, which involve acquiring land or older properties, improving them, and then selling them for a profit. This sector can generate significant returns but also carries higher risks.

Real Estate-Backed Securities: These include investments in CMBS (Commercial Mortgage-Backed Securities) and other debt-based real estate investments. They allow family offices to participate in real estate growth without the direct responsibility of property management.

Advantages of Real Estate Investing for Family Offices

Real estate investments come with a host of benefits that make them attractive to family offices:

Cash Flow Generation: Real estate properties, especially rental properties, generate a reliable stream of income. This steady cash flow can be used for reinvestment or to provide liquidity for other investments or family expenses.

Capital Appreciation: Historically, real estate has been an excellent long-term investment. Property values tend to appreciate over time, providing family offices with significant wealth accumulation opportunities.

Control Over Investments: Family offices enjoy a high degree of control over their real estate investments. They can manage properties, make strategic decisions regarding acquisitions and sales, and tailor their investments to meet specific family goals.

Tax Benefits: Real estate offers various tax advantages, such as depreciation, which allows for the deduction of property depreciation against taxable income. Additionally, 1031 exchanges allow family offices to defer capital gains taxes when selling one property and reinvesting the proceeds into another property.

Community Impact: Family offices can use their investments to improve communities, such as by revitalizing distressed neighbourhoods or investing in social housing, which can increase the family's goodwill and public reputation.

Diversification: Adding real estate to a family office's portfolio offers a valuable layer of diversification. Since real estate performs differently from stocks and bonds, it can help reduce overall risk, especially in volatile markets.

Real Estate Investments Before, During, and After the COVID-19 Pandemic

The COVID-19 pandemic significantly impacted the global real estate market, causing changes in both demand and supply. The dynamics of real estate investments shifted considerably, affecting decision-making processes in family offices:

Before the Pandemic: Prior to the pandemic, real estate was considered a stable and predictable asset class. Residential properties, in particular, were sought after for steady rental income. Commercial real estate also attracted attention due to long-term lease agreements that provided a reliable revenue stream.

During the Pandemic: The pandemic led to shifts in demand. Office spaces and retail properties were hit hardest, with many businesses opting for remote work and online shopping, respectively. On the other hand, residential real estate remained relatively strong as demand grew for more spacious homes and suburban properties. Industrial properties gained popularity, especially logistics centres and warehouses, as e-commerce activities surged.

After the Pandemic: As economies recover, the real estate sector is adjusting to new demands. There is an increased focus on properties that meet the needs of remote workers, such as suburban homes and multi-functional spaces. Commercial spaces are being reimagined with a focus on flexible office spaces and mixed-use developments that cater to post-pandemic lifestyles. There is also a growing emphasis on sustainability and PropTech (property technology) as more people prioritize eco-friendly living and smart technologies in buildings.

Why Family Offices Are Betting Big on Real Estate

Family offices are increasingly betting on real estate as a key asset class. Real estate offers a mix of benefits, from capital appreciation and rental income to portfolio diversification and tax benefits. Family offices are drawn to this sector for various reasons:

Diversification: Real estate is a valuable component of a diversified portfolio, offering a hedge against financial market volatility.

Long-Term Growth: The long-term growth potential of real estate is appealing to family offices looking to preserve and grow wealth across generations.

Stable Income: Rental properties and real estate funds provide a consistent income stream, making them attractive for family offices that prioritize financial stability.

Technological Innovations: Family offices are increasingly investing in PropTech startups, which are revolutionizing property management, transactions, and real estate development. These innovations offer both operational efficiencies and high returns.

8. Alternate Investment Fund (AIF)

Alternative Investment Funds (AIFs) invest in assets not part of traditional investments like stocks, bonds, and cash. They provide specialised investment opportunities, often promising higher returns, but they are designed for sophisticated investors who are willing to invest a higher amount, typically ₹1 crore or more. These funds have grown rapidly in India in recent years, expanding by more than ten times over the past seven years. The total assets under management in this space have reached ₹7 trillion as of the latest reports from the Indian Association of Alternative Investment Funds (IAAIF). AIFs typically have a long-term horizon, often spanning 10 years, which means they require ongoing involvement from financial advisors to manage investor expectations.

AIFs in Real Estate Financing

AIFs have become an important source of funding for the Indian real estate market. They play a key role in financing delayed or stalled projects and contribute to the overall growth of both the residential and commercial real estate sectors. In the past year, the residential market has seen significant improvements, and commercial real estate has benefitted from increased demand in retail and office space. AIFs are also supporting the development of commercial and residential projects, contributing to market liquidity and professionalizing the sector. Domestic and international investors are actively involved, and the regulatory framework is supportive of the growth of AIFs in this space.

The key to a robust and balanced investment portfolio lies in diversification across various asset classes. Real estate AIFs offer an attractive proposition for investors looking to diversify beyond traditional investment options like equities and gold. By adding real estate to their investment mix, investors can create a more robust portfolio that is less susceptible to the inherent volatility of the stock market. Additionally, real estate investments often exhibit low correlation with other asset classes, thereby acting as a hedge against market downturns. Investing in real estate AIFs in India can help diversify HNI portfolios. These fund platforms provide SEBI-approved access to diverse and lucrative asset classes within the real estate sector. The potential for rental yields, whether through commercial or industrial investments, helps by adding steady rental income for investors to complement sales-oriented residential strategies. Moreover, real estate AIFs complement traditional investment portfolios, offering the much-needed diversification required for long-term wealth creation.

The Role of AIFs in Housing and Commercial Real Estate

AIFs have the potential to bring much-needed liquidity to the real estate sector, particularly for stalled or delayed projects. They are also playing a crucial role in the development of both residential and commercial properties. With increasing institutional investment and greater confidence from stakeholders, AIFs are set to further revolutionize the Indian real estate sector in the coming years.

An attractive aspect of real estate AIFs is their potential to generate regular income through both residential sales revenues and commercial rental yields. Residential AIFs offer investors an attractive blend of both unit sales revenues and capital appreciation over project life spans. At the same time, investors can access steady commercial rental yields via AIFs. A report by Knight Frank indicates that India offers among the highest global yields in commercial real estate, with rental yields between ~8-11% per annum. Whether a fund invests in commercial properties, such as office spaces and shopping complexes, or industrial assets such as warehouses, rental income serves as a stable source of cash flow for investors to supplement residential sales-based strategies.

Regulatory Framework and Development

The Securities and Exchange Board of India (SEBI) introduced the AIF Regulations in 2012 to provide a structured policy framework for private capital pools in India. These regulations were updated in 2022 to further strengthen India's position as an attractive destination for both domestic and international investments. The regulatory developments are crucial for sustaining the growth of the AIF industry and ensuring that it remains competitive on the global stage.

Growth and Challenges in the AIF Industry

The AIF industry in India is expanding rapidly, driven by the increasing participation of domestic investors. Investment is flowing into tier II and III cities, allowing small businesses in these regions to access capital. The startup ecosystem has also seen a major boost, leading to wealth creation across various sectors. Despite these positive developments, the distribution costs associated with AIFs remain high, which poses a challenge for both investors and fund managers. Efforts to streamline these costs and enhance the efficiency of the distribution process, particularly through digital platforms, are critical for the future of AIFs in India.

The Shift in Investor Demographics

Historically, the primary investors in AIFs were Foreign Institutional Investors (FIIs). However, in recent years, there has been a marked shift toward domestic investors, who now contribute 80-90% of the funds raised. This change reflects the growing interest from Indian investors in alternative investment avenues. The increasing participation of domestic investors in AIFs is seen as a step toward diversifying the investor base, moving away from the reliance on foreign capital, and contributing to the overall growth of the Indian investment market. As a result, AIFs are set to play a significant role in India's capital markets, possibly competing with the ₹46 trillion mutual fund industry in the future.

Categories of AIFs

AIF's can be classified into three main categories, each with different investment strategies and goals. These categories are designed to cater to a range of investors seeking different types of investment opportunities. Below is an outline of the categories:

Category I AIFs

Category I AIFs are aimed at supporting investments in start-ups, small and medium enterprises (SMEs), social ventures, and other businesses that align with government or regulatory objectives. These funds are seen as beneficial for fostering innovation and development in sectors that can drive economic growth. Subcategories under Category I AIFs include:

- **Venture Capital Funds**: These funds invest in high-growth start-ups with the potential to scale rapidly.
- **Angel Funds**: A subset of venture capital funds that typically invest in early-stage start-ups.
- **Infrastructure Funds**: These funds focus on the development of critical infrastructure like roads, airports, and energy projects.
- **Social Venture Funds**: These funds aim to support businesses addressing social and environmental issues.
- **SME Funds**: These funds invest in small and medium enterprises, supporting their growth and expansion.

Category II AIFs

Category II AIFs typically invest in businesses that require capital for day-to-day operations and development. These funds are focused on more established businesses that may not qualify for Category I funding but still require significant capital for growth. Private equity, real estate funds, and distressed asset funds are examples of Category II AIFs. While these funds offer strong returns, they do not enjoy the same government incentives or concessions as Category I funds.

Category III AIFs

Category III AIFs are more complex, often involving strategies such as leverage and short-selling. These funds engage in a wide range of investment activities and can include hedge funds, private equity investments in public enterprises (PIPE), and other alternative strategies. Like Category II AIFs, these funds do not benefit from specific government incentives, but they are designed for investors who are looking for higher returns through more aggressive strategies.

Real Estate and Infrastructure Funds

Real Estate Funds: These funds provide investors with exposure to the real estate sector without requiring them to directly own property. Real estate funds are increasingly investing in residential and commercial projects, particularly in rapidly growing cities. Prop Tech and advancements in digital technologies have also influenced the real estate investment landscape, providing tools like virtual property tours and data-driven decision-making that make it easier to manage investments in this sector.

Infrastructure Funds: These funds are focused on large-scale infrastructure projects, such as transportation networks, energy systems, and smart city development. As environmental concerns become more prominent, infrastructure funds are also pivoting toward green and sustainable infrastructure projects. This shift aims to address the growing demand for renewable energy and environmentally friendly development.

Venture Capital and Hedge Funds

Venture Capital Funds: Venture capital plays a crucial role in financing start-ups and high-growth companies. These funds are increasingly leveraging AI and data-driven strategies to identify high-potential businesses. By employing advanced algorithms, venture capitalists are refining their investment strategies to ensure that they back the most promising companies with scalable business models.

Hedge Funds: Hedge funds, known for their more complex investment strategies, use a variety of techniques to generate returns. These strategies often include short selling, leverage, and derivatives trading. Hedge funds are also using advanced technologies like AI and machine learning to engage in high-frequency trading, giving them the potential to generate returns in both volatile and stable market conditions.

Emerging Fund Types: Fund of Funds (FoFs)

Fund of Funds (FoFs) is an emerging category within the AIF space. These funds invest in other AIFs, allowing investors to gain exposure to a diversified set of alternative investment strategies. By pooling capital into multiple AIFs, FoFs offer a diversified portfolio that reduces risk. Technology is also playing a significant role in optimizing the management of FoFs, with AI algorithms helping in portfolio selection and risk management to ensure better returns for investors.

Access to Unique Investment Opportunities

Diversification is the cornerstone of successful investing, and real estate AIFs play a crucial role in achieving a balanced portfolio. Real estate AIFs offer access to a diverse range of real estate asset classes, including residential, commercial, and warehousing projects. Investors can gain exposure to a broader real estate portfolio, reducing the risk associated with investing in a single project or asset class. Certain asset classes, such as industrial and commercial, are not easily accessible to retail investors in an individual capacity and are primarily accessed through a fund's investment program. The ability to invest across different asset classes, through regulated AIF platforms, provides risk mitigation and opportunities for attractive returns to investors.

Fuelling the Growth of the Indian Real Estate Sector

The robust growth of India's real estate sector has been significantly bolstered by the emergence of Real Estate Alternative Investment Funds (AIFs). These funds have injected renewed dynamism into the sector by attracting both domestic and foreign investment. AIFs, with their structured approach and focus on transparency and professional management, have not only simplified the investment process but have also catalysed the development of diverse real estate projects, ranging from residential and commercial spaces to industrial projects. The infusion of capital through AIFs has expedited project execution, stimulated economic activity, and contributed to job creation, thereby propelling the growth trajectory of the real estate sector.

The AIF industry in India has shown remarkable growth, with the total commitment to these funds reaching ₹6.4 lakh crore as of March 2022. As the industry matures, continued regulatory support will be essential for unlocking its full potential. With a strong base of domestic investors and a favourable regulatory environment, AIFs offer a promising opportunity for investors seeking to diversify their portfolios and achieve higher returns

Technological Advancements in AIFs

With the rise of technology-driven platforms, AIFs are becoming more accessible and efficient. These platforms are using advanced tools to simplify the investment process and improve transparency. SEBI's regulation, which requires a minimum investment of ₹1 crore, ensures that only sophisticated investors participate. However, technology is streamlining the process and making it easier for investors to engage with AIFs, allowing for more effective risk management and portfolio optimization.

Structure of an AIF

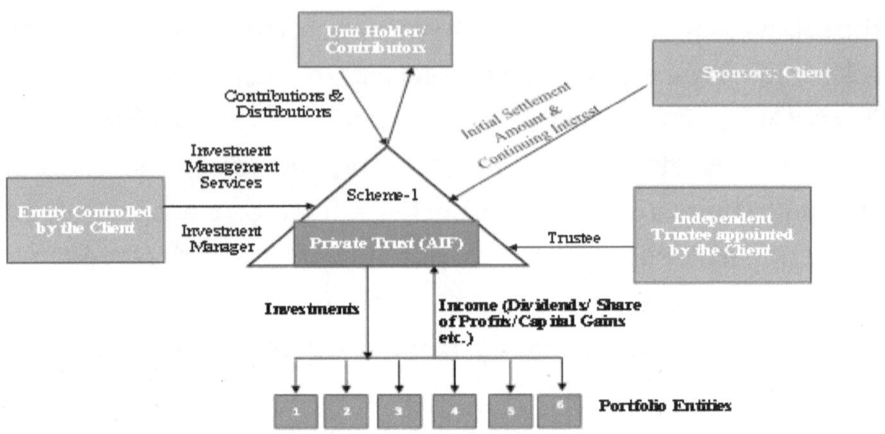

9. Real Estate Investment Trust (REIT)

Real Estate Investment Trusts, commonly known as REITs, are a distinctive and popular investment vehicle. They offer a unique combination of features that make them a compelling choice for investors seeking to tap into the real estate market without the complexities associated with direct property ownership.

At the heart of the REIT concept lies a dedicated focus on real estate. REITs are specialized entities that channel their resources into various types of income-producing real estate assets. These assets can encompass a wide spectrum, ranging from stately office buildings and bustling shopping centres to cozy apartment complexes, luxurious hotels, and essential industrial facilities. Moreover, REITs can also delve into the realm of real estate financing, participating in the ownership of mortgages tied to these properties. This inherent real estate focus ensures that a significant portion of a REIT's revenue is derived directly from the rental income and capital gains generated by these tangible, bricks-and-mortar investments.

They have gained popularity in India as a means of investing in real estate while providing liquidity and diversification to investors. The introduction of REITs in India is relatively recent, with regulatory changes that paved the way for their establishment.

Here are some key points about REITs in India:

Regulatory Framework:

The Securities and Exchange Board of India (SEBI) introduced regulations for REITs in 2014, with subsequent amendments. These regulations govern the formation and operation of REITs in India, ensuring transparency and investor protection.

Structure:

REITs in India are structured similarly to those in other countries. They are typically set up as trusts and are managed by professional asset management companies. The trust holds income-generating real estate properties.

Asset Composition:

Indian REITs primarily invest in income-producing commercial real estate properties. This includes office buildings, shopping malls, IT parks, and other commercial assets. Residential properties were allowed to be included in REIT portfolios starting from 2019.

net distributable income to unit holders. This distribution usually takes the form of dividends.

Liquidity:

Investing in physical real estate properties typically entails substantial upfront capital, along with the potential challenges of illiquidity. However, REITs offer a contrasting advantage in terms of liquidity. These investment vehicles are publicly traded on stock exchanges, rendering the buying and selling of REIT shares a straightforward and accessible process. This liquidity ensures that investors can swiftly adjust their holdings, responding to changing market conditions or capital needs with relative ease. In essence, REITs provide a gateway to the real estate market without the cumbersome limitations of traditional property ownership.

Taxation:

One of the defining features of REITs is their unique tax structure, which offers considerable benefits both to the companies themselves and their shareholders. To maintain this privileged tax status, REITs are required to adhere to specific regulations set forth by the Internal Revenue Service (IRS). Chief among these requirements is the mandate that REITs must distribute at least 90% of their taxable income to their shareholders in the form of dividends. By doing so, REITs can effectively sidestep paying corporate income taxes, thus preserving more of their earnings for distribution to investors. This tax-efficient structure is particularly appealing to investors seeking to maximize their returns while minimizing their tax liability.

Investor Base: Indian REITs attract a wide range of investors, including institutional investors and individual retail investors. They offer a way for retail investors to participate in the commercial real estate market, which was traditionally inaccessible to them due to high capital requirements.

Performance: The performance of Indian REITs can vary based on the quality and location of the underlying properties, economic conditions, and the management of the trust. Investors should conduct thorough research and due diligence before investing in any specific REIT.

Diversification:

Diversification is a fundamental principle of sound investing, and REITs excel in this regard. By investing in a REIT, individuals gain access to a diversified portfolio of real estate assets. These assets span various sectors, from commercial to residential, and often encompass diverse geographical regions. This broad exposure mitigates the risks associated with concentrating investments in a single property or location. Moreover, the diversification provided by REITs allows investors to participate in the growth and performance of different segments of the real estate market, helping to balance the overall risk within their investment portfolio.

Regular Income:

One of the most compelling attractions of investing in REITs is their potential to deliver a consistent stream of income to shareholders. REITs are mandated to distribute a significant portion of their taxable income to investors, resulting in regular dividend payments. These dividends are typically disbursed on a quarterly basis, offering investors a dependable source of income. Moreover, due to the nature of real estate investments and the consistent cash flow generated by rental income, REITs often provide dividend yields that are competitive with other income-generating investments. This reliable income stream can be particularly appealing to investors seeking a steady source of returns to support their financial goals.

REITS and its types

Equity REITs:

Ownership and Management: Equity REITs are perhaps the most common type of REIT. These entities own and actively manage income-producing real estate properties. These properties can encompass a wide range of asset classes, including office buildings, shopping centers, apartment complexes, hotels, industrial facilities, and more.

Income Generation: Equity REITs generate their income primarily through rental income derived from leasing out their real estate properties to tenants. This rental income is a significant source of revenue for these trusts.

Dividend Distribution: As required by law, equity REITs must distribute at least 90% of their taxable income to shareholders in the form of dividends. This distribution structure makes them particularly appealing to income-focused investors seeking regular and potentially high dividend yields.

Mortgage REITs (mREITs):

Investment Focus: Unlike equity REITs, mortgage REITs do not own physical real estate properties. Instead, they primarily invest in financial instruments related to real estate, such as mortgage-backed securities (MBS) and mortgage loans.

Income Generation: mREITs generate income primarily from the interest earned on their investments in mortgages and MBS. They often borrow money at lower short-term interest rates and invest in higher-yielding mortgage assets, profiting from the interest rate spread.

Risk Profile: mREITs are typically more sensitive to interest rate fluctuations and market volatility because their income and profitability depend on the spread between borrowing costs and the yield on their mortgage assets.

Hybrid REITs:

Combining Strategies: Hybrid REITs, as the name suggests, combine elements of both equity and mortgage REITs. They maintain a diversified portfolio that includes both physical real estate properties and real estate-related loans or securities.

Diversification Benefits: The hybrid approach provides diversification within a single REIT, allowing investors to benefit from potential capital appreciation from property ownership and income generation from financial assets.

Risk Mitigation: By diversifying across asset types, hybrid REITs can potentially mitigate some of the risks associated with pure equity or mortgage REITs.

Investors should carefully consider their investment goals, risk tolerance, and market conditions when choosing between these REIT types. Each type offers a unique risk-return profile, and the performance of a REIT can be influenced by various factors, including economic conditions, interest rates, and the management expertise of the REIT's management team. Additionally, it's crucial to conduct thorough research or seek professional advice before investing in REITs to make informed decisions based on individual financial objectives.

10. Initial Public Offering (IPO)

An IPO (Initial Public Offering) is a significant financial event in the life of a company, marking its transition from a privately held entity to a publicly traded one. This transformative process represents a complex series of actions that a company undertakes to make a portion of its ownership available to the investing public for the very first time. Let's delve deeper into the process and significance of an IPO:

Raising Capital:

The primary objective of an IPO is to raise capital. Companies opt for an IPO when they require substantial funds to finance various strategic initiatives such as expansion, research and development, debt reduction, or acquisitions. By offering shares to investors, the company can access a broader pool of capital than what may be available through private financing.

Public Ownership:

In an IPO, the company sells a portion of its ownership, represented by shares, to a diverse group of investors. This means that individuals and institutional investors, such as mutual funds and pension funds, become part-owners of the company. Public ownership provides liquidity to existing shareholders, allowing them to sell their shares on the open market if they choose to do so.

Underwriters' Role:

Companies typically engage investment banks as underwriters to facilitate the IPO. Underwriters play a pivotal role in determining the offer price at which the shares will be sold to the public. They also assess market demand, structure the offering, and coordinate the sale of shares to institutional and retail investors.

Underwriters provide a degree of certainty to the company by committing to purchase the shares if they are unable to sell them to investors at the offer price. This commitment mitigates the risk associated with the IPO.

Regulatory Compliance:

Going public involves rigorous regulatory compliance. Companies must adhere to a stringent set of rules and regulations set forth by regulatory authorities, such as the Securities and Exchange Board of India (SEBI) in India. Compliance ensures that the offering is conducted transparently and fairly and that investors have access to accurate and complete information.

Offer Price Determination:

One of the crucial steps in an IPO is determining the offer price at which the shares will be sold to investors. This price is often determined through a combination of factors, including financial performance, market conditions, investor sentiment, and the assessment of underwriters. The offer price must strike a balance between raising sufficient capital for the company and being attractive to investors.

Subscription and Allotment:

During the IPO, investors have the opportunity to subscribe to purchase shares at the offer price. The subscription period is a critical phase during which the company gauges demand for its shares. Based on investor interest, shares are allotted to institutional and retail investors.

Stock Exchange Listing:

The successful completion of an IPO results in the company's shares being officially listed on a recognized stock exchange. This means that the shares become tradable, and investors can buy and sell them in the open market. The listing day is a significant moment when the company officially becomes publicly traded.

Ongoing Reporting and Disclosure:

As a publicly traded company, ongoing reporting and disclosure become a part of the company's obligations. It must provide regular financial reports, disclosures, and updates to investors and regulatory authorities. Transparency and timely communication are critical to maintaining investor confidence.

Market Valuation:

The IPO process often determines the market valuation of the company. The share price at which the IPO is offered and the subsequent trading price on the exchange reflect the collective assessment of the company's worth by the investing community. This valuation can impact the company's future financing options, acquisition opportunities, and overall strategic decisions.

The IPO Odyssey:

The odyssey to listing typically commences with a resolute decision by the privately held company to "go public." This entails initiating an IPO, a meticulous, and strictly regulated process through which the company makes its shares available for public purchase for the first time.

Regulatory Rigor:

Regulatory compliance assumes paramount importance in the journey to listing. The company must meticulously adhere to a stringent set of regulatory requisites stipulated by competent authorities, such as India's Securities and Exchange Board of India (SEBI). These prerequisites exist to foster transparency, safeguard investor interests, and ensure the integrity of financial markets.

The IPO's Central Role:

The heart of the listing process lies in the IPO itself, serving as the primary conduit through which the company secures capital from the public. This pivotal event encompasses several critical phases. Preparations entail rigorous financial audits, meticulous compliance evaluations, and the selection of a spectrum of intermediaries, including underwriters, legal advisors, and auditors. The creation of the Red Herring Prospectus (RHP), an exhaustive document divulging intricate insights into the company's business, financial standing, risks, and the IPO offering, is a keystone. Regulatory adherence is scrupulously observed, necessitating approvals from regulatory authorities such as SEBI.

Valuation and Transparency:

Listing bestows the company with a market-determined valuation. The IPO offer price and subsequent trading prices reflect the collective valuation accorded by the investment community. This valuation wields considerable influence over the company's capacity to mobilize capital, negotiate mergers and acquisitions, and make strategic financial choices.

Liquidity and Exit Strategy:

Existing shareholders, including founders, early investors, and employees, benefit from listing as it presents an exit strategy. By selling their shares on the open market, they attain liquidity, thereby materializing the value of their investments.

Investor Diversification:

Listing augments the company's shareholder base, ushering in an assortment of investors encompassing institutional entities, mutual funds, retail investors, and individual shareholders. This diversified ownership contributes to stability and shareholder engagement.

Enhanced Oversight:

As a publicly traded entity, the company becomes subject to rigorous regulatory oversight. Adherence to reporting and disclosure obligations, commitment to corporate governance standards, and responsiveness to regulatory inquiries become integral aspects of the company's modus operandi.

Pre-IPO (Pre-Initial Public Offering):

The Pre-IPO (Pre-Initial Public Offering) phase is a critical stage in the journey of a company that is gearing up to become a publicly traded entity. This period, which precedes the actual IPO, is characterized by intensive preparations and strategic activities aimed at ensuring a smooth and successful transition to the public markets. Let's delve deeper into the significance and key components of the Pre-IPO phase:

Financial Audit and Due Diligence:

One of the foundational steps in the Pre-IPO phase is a comprehensive financial audit and due diligence process. This involves a meticulous review of the company's financial statements, accounting practices, and internal controls. The objective is to ensure that the financial statements are accurate, compliant with accounting standards, and present a true and fair view of the company's financial health.

Due diligence goes beyond financials and encompasses a broader examination of the company's operations, legal compliance, contractual obligations, and potential risks. This exhaustive scrutiny is conducted to identify and rectify any issues that could affect the IPO process or investor confidence.

Selection of Intermediaries:

Engaging the right team of intermediaries is crucial to the success of the Pre-IPO phase. This includes the selection of:

- **Underwriters**: These financial institutions play a central role in helping the company determine the offer price of its shares, assess market demand, and facilitate the sale of shares to institutional and retail investors during the IPO.
- **Legal Advisors:** Legal experts provide guidance on regulatory compliance, corporate governance, contractual obligations, and the preparation of legal documents required for the IPO.
- **Auditors:** Independent auditors review the financial statements to ensure they meet accounting standards and are suitable for public disclosure.

- **Other Specialists:** Depending on the company's specific needs, it may engage other specialists, such as tax advisors or industry consultants, to address specific aspects of the Pre-IPO process.

Drafting the Red Herring Prospectus (RHP):

The Red Herring Prospectus (RHP) is a cornerstone document in the IPO process. During the Pre-IPO phase, the company collaborates with its legal advisors and underwriters to draft this comprehensive disclosure document. The RHP provides potential investors with a detailed understanding of the company, its operations, financial performance, risk factors, and the specifics of the IPO offering.

The RHP serves as a primary source of information for investors to make informed decisions about participating in the IPO. It is a legal document that must adhere to regulatory standards and undergo rigorous review by regulatory authorities like the Securities and Exchange Board of India (SEBI) in India.

Meeting Regulatory Requirements:

A critical aspect of the Pre-IPO phase is ensuring regulatory compliance. Companies must meticulously adhere to the regulatory framework established by authorities like SEBI. This includes satisfying disclosure requirements, governance standards, and transparency obligations. The company also initiates the formal process of obtaining regulatory approvals for the IPO.

Regulatory authorities play a vital role in safeguarding investor interests, and meeting their requirements is essential to proceed with the IPO.

Strategic Planning:

Beyond the technical and compliance aspects, the Pre-IPO phase is an opportune time for strategic planning. Companies may assess their market positioning, evaluate growth opportunities, refine their corporate strategy, and fine-tune their messaging to investors.

Post-IPO (Post-Initial Public Offering):

The Post-IPO (Post-Initial Public Offering) phase is a critical period that follows a company's successful transition from a privately held entity to a publicly traded one through the Initial Public Offering (IPO) process. During this phase, the company undergoes significant changes as it becomes subject to increased regulatory oversight and accountability while also gaining access to the benefits of being a publicly traded company. Let's explore the key components and significance of the post-IPO phase:

Continued Financial Reporting and Disclosure:

A fundamental obligation in the post-IPO phase is the continued financial reporting and disclosure. As a publicly traded company, the company must adhere to stringent reporting standards, including quarterly and annual financial statements. These reports must be accurate, transparent, and compliant with regulatory requirements. The objective is to provide investors with up-to-date information about the company's financial performance, operations, and risks.

Ongoing Communication with Investors and Analysts:

Maintaining an open and transparent line of communication with investors and financial analysts is crucial in the post-IPO phase. Companies often conduct investor relations activities to keep shareholders informed about corporate developments, financial results, and strategic initiatives. Regular earnings calls, investor presentations, and meetings with analysts help foster trust and investor confidence.

Monitoring and Managing Stock Price Performance:

Stock price performance is a key focus in the post-IPO phase. The company and its management closely monitor the trading activity and stock price on the stock exchange. Fluctuations in stock price can be influenced by various factors, including financial results, market conditions, economic trends, and news events. Effective stock price management involves strategies to enhance shareholder value and mitigate volatility.

Implementing Corporate Governance Practices:

Strong corporate governance practices are essential in the post-IPO phase. Companies must establish a board of directors with a balanced mix of independent directors and ensure adherence to corporate governance principles. Governance practices often include the establishment of board committees (e.g., audit, compensation, and nominating committees) and the adoption of policies and procedures to protect shareholder interests.

Utilizing IPO Proceeds:

One of the primary objectives of an IPO is to raise capital, and in the post-IPO phase, the company must strategically utilize the funds raised. The capital can be allocated for a variety of purposes, including:

Business Growth: Funding expansion initiatives, entering new markets, or investing in research and development.

Debt Reduction: Paying down existing debt to improve the company's financial position.

- **Strategic Acquisitions:** Pursuing mergers and acquisitions that align with the company's growth strategy.
- **Working Capital:** Ensuring sufficient liquidity for daily operations and unforeseen expenses.

Adhering to Regulatory Compliance:

Regulatory compliance remains a central aspect of the post-IPO phase. The company must adhere to the ongoing reporting, disclosure, and compliance requirements established by regulatory authorities such as the Securities and Exchange Board of India (SEBI) in India. Failure to meet these obligations can result in regulatory sanctions and loss of investor confidence.

Strategic Decision-Making:

The post-IPO phase presents new opportunities and challenges for the company. With access to public capital markets, the company can consider various strategic options, such as additional equity offerings, debt issuances, or mergers and acquisitions. Strategic decisions must align with the company's long-term goals and enhance shareholder value.

Shareholder Engagement:

Engaging with shareholders is an ongoing endeavour. Companies may conduct shareholder meetings, proxy voting, and initiatives to solicit feedback and address shareholder concerns. Building positive relationships with shareholders fosters trust and support.

FPO (Follow-on Public Offering):

A Follow-on Public Offering (FPO) is a significant financial transaction undertaken by a publicly traded company after its initial public offering (IPO). This strategic move involves the issuance and sale of additional shares to the investing public. FPOs serve as a means for the company to access additional capital beyond what was raised during the IPO. Let's delve deeper into the process and significance of FPOs:

Post-IPO Capital Needs:

Companies often opt for an FPO when they require additional capital to support various strategic initiatives. These needs can include funding for business expansion, research and development, debt reduction, strategic acquisitions, or working capital requirements. The decision to pursue an FPO is influenced by the company's growth objectives and capital requirements.

Issuance of Additional Shares:

In an FPO, the company issues additional shares to the public. These shares can take the form of newly created shares or shares held by existing shareholders who choose to sell their holdings. The company may specify the number of shares to be offered, the offer price, and the terms and conditions of the offering.

Regulatory Approvals:

Similar to an IPO, FPOs are subject to regulatory approvals by authorities such as the Securities and Exchange Board of India (SEBI) in India. Companies must comply with regulatory requirements, including financial reporting, disclosure, and governance standards, to obtain the necessary approvals.

Prospectus or Offer Document:

To facilitate the FPO, the company is required to prepare a prospectus or offer document. This document provides potential investors with comprehensive information about the FPO, the company's financial performance, risk factors, and other essential details. It serves as a critical source of information for investors to make informed decisions about participating in the offering.

Pricing and Allocation:

Determining the offer price for the additional shares is a key aspect of the FPO. The offer price is typically influenced by market conditions, demand for the shares, and the company's valuation. Allocation of shares to investors is also an important consideration, and companies often aim to strike a balance between institutional and retail investors.

Use of Proceeds:

The capital raised through an FPO is expected to be used for the specific purposes outlined in the offering documents. The company must be transparent about how it intends to allocate the proceeds and how they will contribute to the company's growth and financial objectives.

Shareholder Impact:

Existing shareholders may be affected by an FPO. If they choose to participate, their ownership stake in the company may be diluted. Conversely, if existing shareholders do not participate, their ownership percentage in the company will decrease due to the issuance of additional shares.

Timing and Market Conditions:

The timing of an FPO is influenced by market conditions and the company's financial needs. Companies often analyse market trends, investor sentiment, and economic factors to determine the optimal timing for an FPO. It is essential to strike a balance between raising capital when needed and entering the market under favourable conditions.

Post-FPO Implications:

After the FPO is completed, the company continues to operate as a publicly traded entity. It must adhere to ongoing reporting, disclosure, and corporate governance requirements. The company also continues to engage with shareholders and investors to maintain transparency and investor confidence.

Takeaways:

In summary, the process of taking a company from private ownership to public trading involves several distinct phases, each with its own significance and purpose. The first of these phases is the **Listing**, which occurs when a company's shares become available for trading on a stock exchange following its initial public offering (IPO). This marks a pivotal moment in the company's evolution, as it gains access to public capital markets and becomes accountable to a wider range of stakeholders, including investors, regulators, and the general public.

Preceding the Listing is the **Pre-IPO** phase, a preparatory period in which the company readies itself for the IPO. During this phase, extensive due diligence is conducted to ensure accurate financial reporting, and key intermediaries such as underwriters, legal advisors, and auditors are engaged to assist in navigating the complex IPO process. Additionally, the drafting of the Red Herring Prospectus (RHP) and compliance with regulatory requirements, often under the supervision of entities like the Securities and Exchange Board of India (SEBI), are central activities that pave the way for a successful IPO.

The **IPO** itself represents a seminal moment in a company's journey. It involves the initial offering of shares to the public, through which the company raises capital by selling a portion of its ownership in the form of shares to investors. Investment banks typically act as underwriters, guiding the pricing, structuring, and distribution of shares to institutional and retail investors. An IPO provides access to a broader pool of capital, facilitating growth, debt reduction, or other strategic objectives.

Following the IPO, the **Post-IPO** phase ensues, during which the company has officially become publicly traded, and its shares are listed and traded on a stock exchange. Regulatory compliance and continued financial reporting are essential during this phase, ensuring transparency and investor confidence. Ongoing communication with investors and analysts, diligent stock price management, adherence to corporate governance practices, and the strategic deployment of the capital raised in the IPO are all critical elements in the post-IPO phase.

Finally, a **Follow-on Public Offering (FPO)** is a subsequent offering of shares made by a publicly traded company. This comes after the initial IPO and serves as a means to raise additional capital for various purposes, including expansion, debt reduction, or acquisitions. FPOs require regulatory approvals and the preparation of a prospectus or offer document, and they offer companies a strategic opportunity to further leverage the benefits of being publicly traded.

In essence, these phases collectively represent the journey a company undertakes from private ownership to publicly traded status, allowing it to raise capital from the public markets and navigate the complexities and opportunities that come with such a transformation.

A few Case Studies on IPO's:

(i) Embassy Office Park REIT (2019):

The Embassy Office Parks REIT IPO, backed by global private equity firm Blackstone Group LP and Bengaluru-based developer Embassy Property Developments Pvt Ltd, aimed to raise ₹4,750 is a groundbreaking Real Estate Investment Trust (REIT) that has emerged as a transformative force in India's real estate sector. Launched as one of India's first REITs, Embassy Office REIT holds a diversified portfolio of high-quality commercial properties, including office spaces and business parks. This case study delves into the intricate details of Embassy Office REIT, exploring its inception, significance, and impact on India's real estate landscape.

Background and Sponsorship:

As per the update in September 2021, Embassy Office Park REIT had achieved a momentous milestone by successfully raising ₹4,750 crores through its Initial Public Offering (IPO). This event not only marked a significant achievement for the REIT itself but also had profound implications for India's real estate and financial sectors.

Embassy Office Park REIT had emerged as a prominent player in India's Real Estate Investment Trusts (REITs) arena. Its credibility and attractiveness were underpinned by strong sponsorship, with the backing of the renowned Embassy Group, a real estate developer with a track record of delivering top-tier commercial properties. Additionally, a strategic partnership with global investment powerhouse Blackstone further solidified the REIT's standing, positioning it as a formidable entity in the market.

Landmark IPO:

The cornerstone of this development was the landmark IPO that raised ₹4,750 crores. This IPO was notable not only for its substantial size but also for its implications within the Indian real estate and financial landscapes. It underscored the growing recognition of the REIT structure as a robust avenue for raising capital in the real estate sector.

Portfolio and Operations:

Embassy Office Park REIT's strength lay in its diverse and strategically located portfolio of real estate assets. This portfolio encompassed various income-generating properties, including office spaces and business parks, all strategically situated across major Indian cities. These strategic locations were a response to the surging demand for high-quality office spaces in India's urban centers.

The operational model of the REIT revolved around leasing these commercial properties to corporate tenants, a strategy that consistently generated rental income. This income stream formed the bedrock for the REIT's financial performance and played a pivotal role in its commitment to distributing income to unit holders.

Significance and Impact:

The impact of Embassy Office Park REIT's ₹4,750 crores IPO rippled across India's real estate sector and financial markets. The IPO's substantial size and success served as a compelling testament to the efficacy of the REIT structure in mobilizing capital for real estate developers. Moreover, it provided investors with a valuable avenue to participate in India's burgeoning commercial real estate market.

Conclusion:

In summation, Embassy Office Park REIT's triumphant ₹4,750 crores IPO represented a pivotal moment in the annals of India's real estate and financial landscapes. Bolstered by strong sponsorship, a diversified portfolio, and a resolute commitment to income distribution, the REIT epitomized the transformative potential of the REIT structure. Its influence extended beyond the IPO, shaping the evolving dynamics of India's commercial real estate sector and affording investors the opportunity to partake in its growth story. It is important to note that developments may have occurred in Embassy Office Park REIT or the real estate sector since my last update, and it is prudent to refer to current and authoritative sources for the latest information.

(ii) Mindspace Business Parks REIT (2020):

In August 2020, Mindspace Business Parks REIT made a notable debut in India's financial landscape. Sponsored by two prominent entities, K. Raheja Corp and the Blackstone Group, this Real Estate Investment Trust (REIT) marked a significant milestone in the Indian real estate sector and the country's burgeoning REIT market.

Background and Sponsorship: Mindspace Business Parks REIT was introduced to the Indian investment landscape as the second REIT to be listed in the country. Its successful launch was underpinned by the substantial experience and financial acumen of its sponsors. K. Raheja Corp, a renowned real estate developer, and Blackstone Group, one of the world's largest alternative asset managers, jointly sponsored the REIT. Their partnership brought together a wealth of expertise in real estate development, investment management, and market insight.

The Landmark IPO:

One of the defining features of Mindspace Business Parks REIT was its Initial Public Offering (IPO), which garnered significant attention from investors and market observers alike. The IPO was instrumental in raising approximately ₹4,500 crore, a remarkable achievement that underscored the confidence of investors in the Indian REIT market. This sizable capital infusion contributed to the strengthening of the REIT's financial position and its ability to pursue strategic objectives.

Portfolio and Operations:

At its core, Mindspace Business Parks REIT is a property trust that owns and operates a diverse portfolio of office properties strategically located in key Indian cities. These commercial assets are meticulously curated to cater to the evolving needs of modern businesses. The REIT's properties serve as contemporary, efficient, and dynamic workspaces that align with the requirements of today's corporate tenants.

Mindspace Business Parks REIT's properties are not merely bricks and mortar; they are hubs of economic activity, fostering innovation and collaboration among businesses. The portfolio's geographic diversity, encompassing prominent Indian cities, positions the REIT as a compelling choice for enterprises seeking prime office spaces in these thriving urban centres.

Significance and Impact:

The introduction of Mindspace Business Parks REIT in India in 2020 held immense significance for multiple stakeholders. For investors, it presented an opportunity to participate in the real estate sector's growth while enjoying the liquidity and transparency of a publicly traded entity. The REIT structure provided an avenue for stable income generation, potential capital appreciation, and diversification within investment portfolios.

On the corporate front, Mindspace Business Parks REIT's presence and offerings addressed the evolving workspace preferences of businesses, especially in light of changing dynamics driven by technology, globalization, and the demand for flexible office solutions. The REIT's properties supported the operational needs and growth aspirations of numerous companies, contributing to economic development and job creation in the regions where its properties were located.

Conclusion:

In conclusion, the debut of Mindspace Business Parks REIT in August 2020 marked a significant juncture in India's real estate and financial markets. It exemplified the potential of REITs as a compelling investment vehicle and showcased the trust and confidence of investors in this asset class. Through its strategic portfolio of office properties and the combined expertise of its sponsors, the REIT played a pivotal role in shaping the landscape of modern workspaces in India while offering investors an attractive avenue for participation in the real estate sector's growth.

(iii) Brookfield India Real Estate Trust (2020):

In February 2020, the launch of the Brookfield India Real Estate Trust marked a significant milestone in the Indian real estate landscape. Sponsored by Brookfield Asset Management, one of the world's largest alternative asset managers, this Real Estate Investment Trust (REIT) made a substantial impact on the Indian capital market. This case study explores the details and significance of this landmark REIT and its influence on the Indian real estate sector.

Background and Sponsorship:

Brookfield Asset Management, a global leader in alternative investments, played a pivotal role as the sponsor of the Brookfield India Real Estate Trust. With a distinguished track record in real estate investments and asset management, Brookfield brought extensive expertise and financial acumen to the Indian market. The trust was structured to leverage Brookfield's vast experience in managing real estate assets across the globe.

The Pathbreaking IPO:

One of the defining features of the Brookfield India Real Estate Trust was its Initial Public Offering (IPO), which took place in February 2020. The IPO was instrumental in raising approximately ₹3,800 crore, making it a substantial entry into the Indian REIT market. This successful capital infusion underscored the confidence of investors in the potential of Indian real estate and the attractiveness of the REIT as an investment avenue.

Diversified Real Estate Portfolio:

At its core, the Brookfield India Real Estate Trust is a vehicle for investors to participate in a diversified portfolio of commercial real estate assets located across major Indian cities. The trust's portfolio includes a mix of office spaces, technology parks, and other commercial properties. This diversification mitigates risk and aligns with the evolving demand for high-quality commercial real estate in India's growing urban centres.

Strategic Significance:

The introduction of the Brookfield India Real Estate Trust in India carried profound implications for various stakeholders. For investors, it offered an opportunity to access the potential of Indian real estate markets while enjoying the liquidity and transparency that come with publicly traded entities like REITs. The trust provided a platform for stable income generation and potential capital appreciation, diversifying investment portfolios.

From a corporate perspective, the trust's presence and portfolio addressed the evolving needs of businesses for modern, well-equipped office spaces. As the Indian economy continued to grow and attract global companies, the trust's assets contributed to supporting the operational requirements of various businesses, fostering economic development and job creation in the regions where its properties were located.

Conclusion:

In conclusion, the launch of the Brookfield India Real Estate Trust in February 2020 represented a significant development in India's real estate and financial markets. It exemplified the potential of REITs as a compelling investment vehicle and showcased the trust and confidence of investors in this asset class. Through its diversified portfolio of commercial real estate assets and the global expertise of its sponsor, the trust played a pivotal role in shaping

India's commercial real estate landscape while offering investors a unique avenue for participation in the sector's growth.

(iv) Macrotech Developers Limited (formerly Lodha Developers) (2021):

In April 2021, Macrotech Developers Limited, formerly known as Lodha Developers, embarked on a significant journey in the Indian real estate sector by launching its Initial Public Offering (IPO). Macrotech Developers is recognized as one of India's largest and most prominent real estate developers, and its IPO was poised to make a significant impact in the industry. This case study delves into the details of this landmark IPO and its strategic significance.

Background and Evolution:

Macrotech Developers has established a formidable presence in India's real estate landscape, with a history of delivering high-quality residential and commercial projects. The company's journey from its inception to its decision to go public in 2021 was marked by its commitment to innovation, excellence in construction, and customer-centric approach. The decision to conduct an IPO was driven by strategic imperatives, including the need for capital infusion for debt reduction and further project development.

The IPO as a Capital Raising Tool:

The primary objective of Macrotech Developers' IPO was to raise capital. Specifically, the company sought to reduce its debt burden, which is common in the capital-intensive real estate sector, and channel funds toward project development. Debt reduction is a key priority for real estate developers as it enhances financial stability and reduces interest costs, thereby improving profitability and risk management.

Substantial Offering and Market Attention:

Macrotech Developers' IPO was substantial in terms of both its offering size and the attention it received in the Indian capital markets. The Rs 3,500 crore IPO garnered considerable interest from investors, reflecting their confidence in the company's reputation and the potential of the Indian real estate sector. The IPO's success hinged on various factors, including the timing of the offering, market sentiment, and the company's ability to communicate its growth strategy effectively.

Utilizing IPO Proceeds:

The capital raised through the IPO was earmarked for specific purposes. Debt reduction was a primary focus, as it contributes to a healthier balance sheet and lower financial risk. By reducing debt, Macrotech Developers aimed to strengthen its financial position and improve its credit profile. Additionally, the company intended to allocate funds to project development, which is integral to its growth strategy. These funds would be used to initiate, complete, and market new real estate projects, thereby expanding the company's portfolio and market presence.

Strategic Impact and Industry Influence:

Macrotech Developers' decision to go public was not only significant for the company itself but also for the Indian real estate sector. It showcased the sector's ability to attract capital from the public markets and highlighted the confidence of investors in established players. Moreover, the IPO signaled the company's commitment to transparency, corporate governance, and investor engagement, aligning with the evolving expectations of investors and regulators.

Conclusion:

In conclusion, Macrotech Developers Limited's IPO in April 2021 represented a pivotal moment in the company's journey and a significant development in India's real estate industry. It underscored the strategic importance of accessing public capital markets to address financial priorities, such as debt reduction and project development. The IPO's success and market attention demonstrated the resilience and potential of the Indian real estate sector, while also emphasizing the company's commitment to transparency and responsible corporate governance. Macrotech Developers embarked on a new chapter in its growth trajectory, leveraging the capital raised through the IPO to further shape India's real estate landscape.

Chapter 4

SPECIALISED FINANCING TOOLS FOR DEVELOPERS

1. Lease Rental Discounting (LRD)

What is Lease Rental Discounting (LRD)?

Lease Rental Discounting (LRD) is a form of financing where developers can obtain loans by using the rental receipts of their commercial properties as collateral. In India, this method is increasingly used by property developers who own income-generating assets such as office buildings, retail outlets, and warehouses. The loan amount is determined based on the long-term cash flows from rental payments, and this loan is typically repaid using the rents received from tenants over the lease period.

Factors Considered by a Bank When Making a Loan

When applying for an LRD loan, the bank will evaluate several factors to determine the loan amount and eligibility. These include:

1. **Property Worth**: The market value of the developer's commercial property is a critical factor. Properties with a high rental yield are more likely to receive a larger loan amount.
2. **Repayment Capacity**: The developer's ability to repay the loan from the rental income generated by the property is assessed.
3. **Other Properties**: If the developer has additional properties or assets, these can strengthen the loan application.
4. **Property's Legality and Technical Aspects**: The legal standing and technical aspects of the property, such as ownership rights and the quality of infrastructure, are carefully scrutinized.
5. **Potential Liabilities**: The bank also considers any outstanding liabilities or encumbrances on the property that could impact repayment.

How Does Lease Rental Discounting (LRD) Function?

In the context of Indian real estate, **LRD loans** allow developers to leverage their leased properties as collateral for financing. The tenant signs a lease agreement to pay regular rent for the property, and these lease receipts serve as a reliable source of income for repaying the loan. Banks or financial institutions then grant loans based on the rental income stream, providing developers with liquidity while retaining ownership of their properties.

Eligibility for LRD in India

Developers in India who own income-generating properties can apply for LRD loans. The eligibility extends to:

- **Salaried Individuals**: Developers or business owners with a steady income source can access LRD.

- **Self-Employed Individuals and Professionals**: Self-employed developers, including those in the real estate sector, are eligible.
- **Non-Individual Entities**: These include partnership firms, private and public limited enterprises, and proprietorship firms in real estate development.

Benefits of Lease Rental Discounting for Developers

- **Business Expansion**: LRD provides developers with funds to invest in additional properties, aiding in the expansion of their real estate portfolios.
- **Tax Benefits**: Developers can benefit from tax advantages by owning more property, as rental income is generally treated favourably for tax purposes.
- **Balanced Cash Flow**: Developers can maintain a balanced cash flow, as loan repayments are linked to rental receipts, making them easier to manage. This can be particularly useful for developers managing multiple ongoing projects.
- **Low Capital Expenditure**: LRD allows developers to obtain capital without requiring significant upfront personal investment. This enables them to invest in new projects or property acquisitions while minimizing financial strain.
- **Top-Up Funding**: Developers can also use LRD to top-up their funding needs if they have previously used loans or if their rental income has increased.

2. Inventory Financing

Inventory Financing is a form of short-term financing where businesses, including real estate developers, leverage their unsold or ready-to-occupy inventory as collateral to obtain financial assistance. This financing mechanism provides developers with quick access to liquidity, which is particularly useful during periods when a significant portion of their inventory remains unsold. Inventory financing is crucial for real estate developers in India, especially when facing slow-moving sales and financial strain due to unsold units.

This financing option helps developers bridge cash flow gaps, reduce debt burden, and continue operations without resorting to asset liquidation. In the real estate sector, unsold inventory can become a significant challenge due to slow sales, delayed payments, or market downturns.

What Developers Get from Banks in India

Real estate developers in India generally seek inventory financing from commercial banks or NBFCs (Non-Banking Financial Companies). While specific offerings vary by institution, the general structure of inventory financing typically includes the following elements:

Loan Amount:

Banks typically provide financing against unsold or ready-to-sell inventory. The loan amount is often based on the market value of the inventory and is usually determined by an independent valuation of the unsold properties. Banks generally offer up to 50% to 70% of the realisable value of the unsold units as the loan amount.

Loan Tenure:

The loan is generally a short-term loan, with a typical tenure ranging from 6 months to 3 years. This tenure depends on the expected time frame for the developer to liquidate the inventory or the project's cash flow cycle.

Loan-to-Value (LTV) Ratio:

Banks offer a Loan-to-Value (LTV) ratio, which is usually between 50% and 70% of the current market value of the unsold units. In some cases, if the project has high-quality inventory (such as premium apartments or commercial units), the LTV could be as high as 80%. However, the LTV tends to be lower for projects in slower markets or areas with low demand.

Eligibility Criteria:

- Banks typically require developers to have a strong track record in the real estate sector, generally demanding at least 3-5 years of experience in completing residential or commercial projects.
- The developer should have completed a substantial portion of the project and should have a proven sales record or should have sold a certain percentage of the available inventory (usually around 50% to 75%).
- The inventory must be RERA-compliant and free from encumbrances. The loan may also be contingent on the developer's creditworthiness and past financial performance.

Security and Guarantees:

The loan is primarily secured by the unsold inventory itself, with banks requiring the developer's personal guarantees or corporate guarantees from other entities in the group. In some cases, banks may ask for pledge of shares, mortgages of land parcels, or additional collateral if the inventory is not considered high-value enough.

Interest Rates:

The interest rate for inventory financing is typically higher than traditional long-term loans due to the short-term nature and higher risk involved. Rates usually range from 12% to 14% per annum, though they can vary depending on the bank's assessment of the project and the developer's financial standing. Interest payments are typically made monthly, and the principal repayment is linked to the liquidation of the unsold inventory.

Repayment Structure:

The repayment structure is typically linked to sales proceeds from the unsold inventory. Developers are expected to repay the loan amount once the units are sold, or they may repay based on the realization from the sale of each unit. In some cases, a bullet repayment structure may be applied, where the full loan amount is paid back at the end of the tenure.

Sanction Process:

The sanction process involves a thorough project appraisal, which includes an independent valuation of the unsold inventory, an assessment of the project's financial health, and an evaluation of the market conditions. Banks also scrutinize the sales track record, project completion status, and any outstanding liabilities on the project before approving the loan.

Advantages of Inventory Financing for Developers

- **Improved Cash Flow**: Inventory financing provides developers with immediate access to cash, which can help cover operating costs, service debts, or finance the construction of new projects. This is particularly helpful during periods of slow sales when liquidity is often tight.

- **Debt Reduction**: By using inventory financing, developers can use the loan to pay off high-cost debt, thus reducing their interest burden and improving their overall financial standing. It also allows developers to avoid using equity or selling assets at a loss.
- **Flexibility**: Inventory financing offers more flexibility than traditional bank loans, as the developer can repay the loan once the inventory is sold or as the payments are realized from the sales of units. This makes it a useful tool during times when sales cycles are unpredictable.
- **Preservation of Ownership**: Unlike selling inventory at discounted prices or auctioning units, inventory financing allows developers to maintain ownership of their unsold units until the right market conditions arise for sale.
- **Fast and Convenient**: Compared to long-term loans or equity financing, inventory financing is relatively quick and simple to obtain. Developers can access the funds they need to continue project operations and other capital needs without lengthy approval processes.

Challenges with Inventory Financing in Real Estate

- **High Interest Rates**: Inventory financing is typically offered at higher interest rates (12-14% annually) compared to regular commercial loans or long-term financing options. This can increase the overall financial burden on developers, particularly if the inventory takes a long time to sell.

- **Pressure to Sell**: Since inventory financing is tied to the sale of the inventory, developers are under pressure to sell the units quickly. If the market conditions are unfavourable or the inventory takes longer to sell than expected, developers may face difficulties repaying the loan.
- **Dependency on Market Conditions**: The success of inventory financing is heavily reliant on favourable market conditions. If there is a slowdown in real estate demand or significant price fluctuations, it could affect the ability to sell the unsold inventory and repay the loan.
- **Collateral Limitations**: The value of the collateral (unsold units) may fluctuate, especially if the market experiences a downturn. Banks may require **additional collateral** or impose stricter terms if they perceive a higher risk in the project.

3. Last-Mile Funding

Last-mile funding is a type of short-term financing specifically designed to help developers complete **near-finished or stalled projects**. These are projects where most of the construction work has been completed, typically over 70-80%, but are unable to progress further due to financial constraints.

The objective of this funding is to provide the necessary capital to cover the costs of final-stage construction activities, enabling developers to deliver completed units to homebuyers or investors.

In the introduction of the Real Estate (Regulation and Development) Act (RERA) has further emphasized the need for timely project completion, making last-mile funding an indispensable tool for developers facing liquidity issues.

Structure of Last-Mile Funding in India

The structure of last-mile funding in India varies depending on the financier, the stage of the project, and the developer's financial health. Below are the key components of how last-mile funding works:

Purpose of Funding:

- Cover remaining construction costs.
- Pay off pending dues to vendors, contractors, or suppliers.
- Obtain necessary regulatory clearances or permissions.
- Address delays caused by legal or administrative issues.

Eligible Projects:

- Projects that are **70-90% complete** and face a temporary cash flow crisis.
- Stalled projects with potential to generate sales or income once completed.
- RERA-registered projects, as these have better transparency and compliance.

Loan Amount:

The loan amount is typically based on the remaining construction cost and expected cash inflows after project completion. Financiers may offer up to 50-75% of the remaining project cost or more, depending on the viability and demand for the project.

Tenure:

Last-mile funding is usually offered as short-term funding, with a tenure of 6 months to 3 years. The repayment tenure is tied to the expected cash inflows from the project after completion.

Interest Rates:

Interest rates for last-mile funding are typically higher than regular project loans, ranging from 12-18% per annum, depending on the developer's creditworthiness and the project's potential.

Collateral:

Developers must pledge the remaining project inventory, receivables from sold units, or other assets as collateral for the loan. In some cases, lenders may require additional security, such as land parcels or personal guarantees.

Repayment Structure:

The repayment is often linked to project milestones or cash inflows from the sale of completed units. Financiers may also use an escrow mechanism, ensuring that all revenue generated from the project is directed toward loan repayment.

Sanction Process:

The process involves a detailed appraisal of the project, including an assessment of construction status, estimated completion costs, sales potential, and market demand. Lenders also evaluate the developer's track record, financial stability, and adherence to regulatory norms.

Benefits of Last-Mile Funding for Developers

- **Ensures Project Completion**: Last-mile funding helps developers overcome liquidity challenges and complete stalled projects, ensuring timely delivery to homebuyers.
- **Builds Market Credibility**: Delivering projects on time enhances the developer's reputation and builds trust among buyers and investors, which is crucial for future projects.

- **Unlocks Revenue Potential**: Completion of the project allows developers to monetize unsold inventory, recover receivables from sold units, and generate revenue to service debts.
- **Prevents Legal Issues**: Stalled projects often lead to legal disputes and penalties under RERA. Last-mile funding helps avoid these issues by ensuring timely delivery.
- **Revives Buyer Confidence**: Timely completion of projects restores confidence among homebuyers, which is essential for the overall health of the real estate market.

Challenges and Risks in Last-Mile Funding

- **High Interest Costs**: The high interest rates associated with last-mile funding can increase the overall financial burden on developers, especially if sales are slower than anticipated.
- **Market Dependency**: The success of last-mile funding depends on the ability to sell unsold inventory. A weak market or unfavorable economic conditions can impact cash flows and repayment.
- **Limited Collateral**: Developers with limited assets or heavily encumbered projects may struggle to secure last-mile funding due to insufficient collateral.
- **Lender Caution**: Financiers are often cautious about lending to projects with unclear demand or legal complications, which can limit access to last-mile funding.
- **Regulatory Scrutiny**: Projects that are not RERA-compliant or have unresolved disputes may face difficulties in obtaining last-mile funding.

4. Mezzanine Financing - Bridging Debt and Equity

Mezzanine financing is a hybrid funding instrument that combines elements of debt and equity. It serves as an intermediate layer in the capital structure, ranking below senior debt but above common equity. By offering features like interest payments and potential equity participation, mezzanine financing fills the funding gap between traditional debt and equity, providing developers with an essential tool for flexible and strategic project financing.

Primary Uses in Real Estate Development

Mezzanine financing is particularly popular in real estate for projects requiring substantial capital but facing funding gaps. Developers utilize this tool for purposes like project expansion, land acquisition (indirectly), redevelopment projects, and last-mile funding to complete construction. By providing this intermediate funding layer, mezzanine financing enables developers to move forward with projects that might otherwise stall due to insufficient capital.

Key Features of Mezzanine Financing

Subordinated Debt

Mezzanine financing is subordinate to senior debt, meaning that in the event of a default, mezzanine lenders are repaid only after senior lenders have been satisfied. This positioning makes it riskier for lenders but also offers higher returns as compensation for the increased exposure.

Equity Participation

A unique aspect of mezzanine financing is the equity-linked component. Lenders may receive equity options, such as warrants or conversion rights, to convert their investment into an ownership stake under specific conditions. This feature ensures additional returns beyond the interest payments and aligns lender interests with the project's success.

High Returns

To offset the higher risks associated with being subordinate in the repayment hierarchy, mezzanine financing typically offers returns that are higher than senior debt but lower than pure equity returns. These can take the form of fixed interest, profit sharing, or equity-linked gains.

Flexibility

Mezzanine loans are highly customizable, allowing developers to negotiate terms like deferred payments, balloon repayments, or tailored interest structures. This flexibility helps developers manage cash flow effectively throughout the project lifecycle.

Advantages of Mezzanine Financing

Fills Funding Gaps

For developers, mezzanine financing is invaluable in addressing the shortfall between the senior debt offered by banks and the equity they can raise. This ensures that projects remain fully funded without delays.

Minimizes Equity Dilution

Unlike pure equity financing, mezzanine funding allows developers to secure necessary capital without giving up significant ownership or control over the project. This makes it an attractive option for those looking to maintain decision-making power.

Faster Loan Approvals

Given its tailored nature, mezzanine financing typically involves shorter processing times compared to traditional bank loans, enabling developers to act quickly on opportunities.

Supports Riskier Projects

Mezzanine financing is more accommodating for projects with higher perceived risks, such as those in early development phases or in markets with volatile demand. Lenders mitigate these risks through higher interest rates and equity participation.

Challenges of Mezzanine Financing

Higher Cost

The cost of mezzanine financing is substantially higher than senior debt due to its subordinate position in the repayment hierarchy. Developers must weigh the financial burden of these higher returns against the benefits of accessing additional capital.

Subordination Risk

In the event of financial distress, mezzanine lenders stand behind senior debt holders in the repayment order. This increased risk makes mezzanine financing less secure for lenders and necessitates careful project evaluation.

Complex Structures

The hybrid nature of mezzanine financing, which often includes both debt and equity components, can make negotiations and structuring more complex. Developers must ensure they fully understand the implications of all terms and conditions.

Comparison: Mezzanine vs. Other Financing Options

Aspect	Mezzanine Financing	Senior Debt	Equity Financing
Risk Level	Moderate to High	Low	High
Return on Investment	High	Low to Moderate	Highest
Repayment Priority	After senior debt but before equity	First priority	No repayment; depends on profits
Cost to Borrower	Higher than senior debt, lower than equity	Lowest	Highest (due to equity dilution)
Control for Borrower	Retains more control than equity financing	Full control retained	Often involves dilution of control

This table highlights the position of mezzanine financing within the broader spectrum of funding options, demonstrating its unique value proposition.

Typical Terms of Mezzanine Financing

Loan Tenure

Mezzanine loans typically range from three to seven years, aligning with the project timelines of real estate developments.

Interest Rates

The interest rates for mezzanine financing are generally higher than those of senior debt, ranging between 14% and 20% in the Indian context, depending on market conditions and project risk profiles.

Repayment Structure

Flexibility in repayment is a hallmark of mezzanine financing. Developers may opt for deferred payments or balloon repayments at the end of the loan term, easing short-term cash flow pressures.

Equity Component

Many mezzanine deals include equity-linked instruments like warrants, giving lenders the option to participate in the project's success through future equity ownership.

Regulatory and Market Considerations

RBI Guidelines

The Reserve Bank of India (RBI) governs mezzanine financing operations, particularly when offered by NBFCs. Regulations ensure that the funds are deployed responsibly and prohibit certain uses, such as direct land acquisition financing.

Market Trends

Mezzanine financing is gaining traction in India, especially for affordable housing and redevelopment projects. Its growing popularity is driven by the demand for flexible, mid-tier financing solutions that can adapt to evolving market dynamics.

Global Participation

International investors, private equity firms, and institutional funds frequently engage in mezzanine financing, providing additional capital to the Indian real estate sector and fostering innovation in funding models.

Chapter 5

Government Programs and Incentives

1. Tax Increment Financing (TIF)

Tax Increment Financing (TIF) is a public finance tool designed to encourage redevelopment in areas where development might not otherwise occur due to insufficient infrastructure, low property values, or a lack of investor confidence. It allows governments to fund upfront costs of urban renewal projects by capturing the future incremental increases in tax revenue resulting from improved property values within a defined area.

In India, the adoption of TIF could address critical urban challenges, such as underutilized land in prime locations, unplanned slum settlements, and dilapidated inner-city areas, while promoting equitable growth.

How TIF Works: A Step-by-Step Process

(i) TIF District Designation:

- **Criteria for Selection:** The designated TIF District must be an area with economic potential but hindered by outdated infrastructure, poor amenities, or blight. For example, old industrial belts or informal housing zones could be ideal candidates.

- **Baseline Revenue Determination:** The property tax revenue generated from the area is recorded as a baseline. This ensures accountability and provides a benchmark to measure future incremental revenues.

(ii) Infrastructure Investment:

- **Types of Investments:** These can range from constructing roads, sewage and water systems, and public transport networks to building public parks, schools, and community centres. In India, integrating green technologies like solar panels or rainwater harvesting could further enhance value.
- **Financing Mechanisms:**

  Municipal Bonds: Local governments could issue bonds backed by future tax increments.

  Public-Private Partnerships (PPPs): Developers co-invest in infrastructure improvements, sharing project risks and rewards with the government.

(iii) Incremental Tax Revenue Generation:

- **Revenue Monitoring:** A robust digital system is required to calculate the increase in property values post-development, ensuring transparency and efficiency in tax collection.
- **Long-Term Revenue Growth:** Incremental taxes generated from rising commercial rents, property sales, and

redevelopment projects contribute to a self-sustaining funding cycle.

(iv) Repayment of Initial Investment:

- Funds raised via bonds or loans are repaid using incremental revenues over a pre-determined period, often ranging from 10 to 25 years.

Applicability of TIF in the Indian Market

India's rapid urbanization demands innovative solutions to fund large-scale development. TIF, if implemented effectively, could:

(i) Slum Redevelopment:

- Projects like Dharavi Redevelopment in Mumbai could use TIF to finance public housing, transportation, and sanitation upgrades, attracting private developers to build residential and commercial hubs.
- Such projects would ensure better living standards for residents while unlocking the economic value of prime urban land.

(ii) Smart City Initiatives:

- The Smart Cities Mission could integrate TIF to fund high-tech infrastructure, such as fibre-optic networks, smart grids, and efficient transit systems. This approach would reduce dependence on traditional budgetary allocations.

(iv) Transit-Oriented Development (TOD):

- Metro expansions in cities like Bengaluru, Delhi, and Ahmedabad could be complemented by TIF Districts, where areas around metro stations benefit from new residential and commercial developments. Incremental tax revenue could fund further infrastructure expansions.

Advantages of TIF in India

Reduced Burden on Public Finances:

Governments can defer the financial impact of urban projects by utilizing future tax revenues instead of immediate public funds. This aligns well with India's resource-constrained municipalities.

Attracting Private Investment:

Improved infrastructure makes TIF Districts attractive to developers incentivized to invest in mixed-use developments combining retail, residential, and office spaces.

Sustainable Urban Development:

Focused on strategic regions, TIF promotes planned development, reducing urban sprawl and encouraging efficient land use. This could support India's push for green cities by funding eco-friendly infrastructure.

Improved Public Services:

Redevelopment leads to upgraded civic amenities, including schools, hospitals, and recreational spaces, improving quality of life for residents and enhancing property values.

Challenges and Barriers in India

The implementation of Tax Increment Financing (TIF) in India faces several challenges that need to be addressed for its successful adoption. First, India's fragmented property taxation system, which is managed differently across states and municipalities, complicates the uniform application of TIF. To streamline the process, reforms in tax laws would be required, along with provisions for earmarking incremental revenues specifically for redevelopment projects. Additionally, TIF assumes that property values will increase following redevelopment, but this is heavily dependent on market dynamics. Economic downturns, poor planning, or unforeseen circumstances could result in property values not appreciating as expected, leading to insufficient revenue and potential debt defaults. Another hurdle is political and social resistance, as TIF projects often involve the displacement of communities or businesses to make way for redevelopment. Protests could arise, especially in densely populated areas, unless the process is transparent, and the resettlement is handled fairly with equitable distribution of benefits. Lastly, the administrative capacity of Indian cities to evaluate, implement, and manage TIF projects is often lacking. Many local officials may not have the necessary expertise, and therefore, capacity-building programs would be essential to ensure the effective management of TIF projects.

2. SWAMIH Fund

Special Window for completion of construction of Affordable and Mid-Income Housing Projects also known as SWAMIH FUND

What is SWAMIH Fund?

In November 2019, the central government introduced the 'Special Window for Funding Stalled Affordable and Middle-Income Housing Projects' (SWAMIH) Scheme, with the primary objective of facilitating priority debt financing to complete stalled housing projects within the affordable and middle-income housing sectors. This initiative, designed as a form of 'last mile financing,' is channelled through a Category-II AIF (Alternate Investment Fund) debt fund registered with the Securities and Exchange Board of India (SEBI). Rather than functioning as a conventional lender-borrower relationship, the SWAMIH Fund operates as a strategic partner, acting as a "virtual CFO" for the project, overseeing and guiding its financial and operational processes.

Why was the SWAMIH fund needed?

In a Press Information Bureau release, the central government stated that the SWAMIH fund was launched to provide relief to real estate developers who require funding to complete their unfinished projects and ensure the timely delivery of homes to home-buyers. The scheme is expected to aid the growth of the real estate sector in India. About 1,509 housing projects comprising approximately 4.58 lakh housing units which have been stuck to fulfil the eligibility criteria listed below to benefit from the scheme.

For whom has the fund been conceptualized?

The real estate projects seeking last-mile funding from SWAMIH must be RERA-registered projects that have been stalled due to a lack of adequate funds. They must also fall under the 'Affordable and Middle-Income Project' category. Net-worth-positive projects are also eligible for SWAMIH funding. Finally, each of these projects must be very close to completion. Net-worth positive projects are those projects for which the value of their receivables (debts owed to them by buyers), plus the value of their unsold inventories is greater than their completion costs and outstanding liabilities. The Government has defined an 'affordable and middle-income projects' as those projects in which the flats do not measure more than 200 square metres in carpet area and are priced as below:

- Up to INR 2 crore in the Mumbai Metropolitan Region
- Up to INR 1.5 crore in the National Capital Region, Chennai, Kolkata, Pune, Hyderabad, Bangalore and Ahmedabad
- Up to INR 1 crore in the rest of India

Investors

The Central Government, through the Department of Economic Affairs, is the sponsor of the SWAMIH fund. It has infused INR 10,000 crore in the Fund. The Government seeks to obtain matching contributions from other investors including sovereign wealth funds, domestic pension and provident funds, global pension funds, banks, NBFCs and other institutional investors, to generate a total corpus of INR 25,000 crore.

Progress of the fund disbursal till now

SWAMIH Fund will invest ₹24,151 crore across 252 stalled projects

According to a government statement, around 111 projects have been granted final approval. Investments (deal size) will be ₹10,992 crore, against which the project cost is ₹30,503 crore. Beneficiaries or total units under the investment will be 63,716.

On the other hand, preliminary approval has already been granted for 142 projects, entailing an investment of ₹13,159 crore, where the project cost was ₹36,267 crore, and the number of dwelling units coming up stood at 83,662.

The Fund made its first successful exit in October 2021, the project, which was in Borivali, Mumbai, the Rivali Park residential project was the first to receive funding under the SWAMIH Fund.

Funding Eligibility:

For projects to be eligible for support from the alternative investment debt fund, the Government clarified the 'positive net worth' condition. The Fund will not offer support to ventures that the National Company Law Tribunal (NCLT) heard in the Supreme Court and high courts but will take up others.

The cabinet approved the plan to revitalise the ailing industry, which is expected to provide relief to homebuyers, create jobs, increase cement and steel sales, and boost the economy. Net worth positive denotes that the value of receivables plus unsold inventory should be higher than the project's completion cost and outstanding liabilities.

The SWAMIH scheme applies to projects that meet certain criteria to ensure effective utilization of funds. First, the project must be registered with the state real estate regulatory authority (RERA). It specifically targets projects for middle and low-income groups, with price limits on the unit cost to ensure affordability. For example, in the Mumbai market, the price cap is set at Rs 2 crore, while for cities like Delhi-NCR, Pune, Chennai, Hyderabad, Kolkata, Ahmedabad, and Bengaluru, it is Rs 1.5 crore, and Rs 1 crore for other regions. Additionally, the carpet area of each unit is limited to 200 square meters. Projects must also be net-worth positive, meaning the value of the receivables and unsold inventory should exceed the cost of completion and accrued liabilities. Projects with solvency issues or those considered nonperforming assets, but still positive in net worth, are also eligible. However, projects involved in high court or supreme court litigation are not considered. Finally, the scheme targets projects close to completion, where lack of capital is the primary reason for delay, ensuring that only projects nearing completion benefit from this funding.

Fund Structure:

The Government will serve as the proposed Fund's sponsor and has pledged Rs 10,000 crore. As the investment manager, SBICAP Ventures Ltd will be involved and responsible for fundraising, investments and the fund team's management. In addition to Life Insurance Corporation of India (LIC) and others, the Fund is looking for matching contributions from lenders such as State Bank of India to build a corpus of around Rs 25,000 crore.

The Fund will oversee the disbursement of capital and track projects' execution directly or through third-party providers by the developer. As part of the sanction process, current lenders will be consulted. The investment manager will perform a thorough analysis, including feedback given by external due diligence agencies.

This control process would be part of the developers' contractual agreement. Disbursements will occur only after the completion of documentation.

The Fund expects its assets to be predominantly structured in the form of non-convertible debentures, subject to legal, regulatory or other considerations. The investment manager would assess the returns based on each project's risk profile and details, it said. To determine whether the proposal meets the Fund's investment criteria, the investment manager will conduct an internal financial review, which will be supplemented by external due diligence agencies covering areas such as title, financials, real estate, and legal, among others, as well as consultation with existing lenders. The collection of projects and developers will be responsible for the Fund's investment manager and investment committee.

The financial objectivity of the mechanism will not intervene with investors, including the Government, "he said, adding that the fund's investment objectives will drive the decision."

Special Window

The Union Cabinet, chaired by the Prime Minister, approved the creation of a "Special Window" fund to provide priority debt financing to complete stalled housing projects in the affordable and middle-income housing sectors.

The Government acts as the Fund's sponsor, and the Government's total pledge to be infused will be up to INR 10,000 crore. The Fund will be professionally managed and set up as a Category-II AIF (Alternate Investment Fund) debt fund registered with SEBI.

It is suggested that SBICAP Ventures Limited be hired as the Investment Manager for the first AIF under the Special Window.

In turn, this Fund will offer relief to developers who need financing to complete a set of unfinished projects and ensure that home buyers are supplied with homes.

Since the real estate industry is fundamentally connected to a range of other industries, growth in this sector would also positively impact stress relief in other major sectors of the Indian economy.

The unique window's emphasis would be on projects that are delayed because of the lack of funding for construction, it said. Projects where the restructuring plan has not been accepted or rejected by the committee of creditors under the insolvency resolution procedure will not be considered.

The "very close to completion" projects would have priority, it said. The Fund does not accept ventures that require fraud or diversion. As per average risk, there will be caps at the project, developer and city levels.

With the Government providing monetary support through its alternative investment fund to as many as 33 housing projects, over 25,000 stuck housing units will likely be completed soon. According to the finance minister, a Rs 4,197 crore investment has received final approval through the Special Window for Affordable and Mid-Income Housing (SWAMIH) fund. The FM said this Fund would contribute to the construction of 25,048 housing units in a tweet on October 8, 2020.

The Fund was formed in November 2019 to assist RERA-registered stuck projects in India's major housing markets after obtaining approval from the union cabinet. The Fund's monetary support will result in over 60,000 units being built across prime residential markets, including the Metropolitan Area of Mumbai, Chennai, Bengaluru, the National Capital Region and Pune. The SWAMIH fund will also provide liquidity to pending housing projects in Maharashtra, Chandigarh, Uttar Pradesh, Haryana, and Rajasthan.

Loan Restructuring

Retail loans issued to consumers in qualifying stalled projects will be restructured by Reserve Bank of India (RBI) guidelines and bank board-approved policies.

"Since the real estate industry is fundamentally related to a range of other industries, growth in this sector would also have a positive impact on stress relief in other major sectors of the Indian economy," the Government said.

To get through the current situation, cash flow planning and debt commitment structuring are critical. This would include the drawing up of a crisis management strategy and cash situation stress testing. Close project monitoring, post-moratorium options discussion with lenders and exploration of rescue/revival capital for stressed projects will also be required.

Investment Committee:

An investment committee makes the SWAMIH Fund's investment and divestment decisions ("IC"). The IC is made up of SVL team members as well as independent members. The IC must always have a minimum of four members and a maximum of seven members. Investment proposals submitted on behalf of the Fund are forwarded to the IC for final approval. The IC makes investment decisions unanimously. The Investment Manager may alter, replace, or reassemble the IC members (except the CIO).

Advisory Board:

The Investment Manager has formed an advisory board comprised of investor representatives (the "Advisory Board"). As a Contributor, the Government of India is entitled to up to two seats on the Advisory Board, which will be available to one nominee from each of the (i) Department of Economic Affairs, and (ii) the Department of Financial Services, under the Ministry of Finance, Government of India. Other Contributors who have made a Capital Commitment to the Fund each have one seat on the Advisory Board.

The Advisory Board shall:

- Examine potential conflicts of interest and approve or disapprove of them. If the Advisory Board does not give the Fund its permission to invest, the Fund will not be permitted to make such an investment.

- Examine and approve the interim and permanent CIO appointments.
- Provide any advice requested by the Investment Manager.

3. Grants and Subsidies

Grants and Subsidies for Indian Developers

Grants and subsidies play a critical role in supporting the growth and development of the Indian real estate sector, especially for affordable housing projects, green buildings, and urban infrastructure projects. These financial incentives are typically provided by the government to encourage developers to undertake projects that align with national priorities, such as addressing the housing shortage, promoting sustainable construction practices, and enhancing urban infrastructure.

- **Affordable Housing Subsidies**: The government has introduced several subsidies aimed at promoting affordable housing for low- and middle-income groups. Under the **Pradhan Mantri Awas Yojana (PMAY)**, developers are offered various incentives for constructing affordable homes. These include interest subsidies for homebuyers and financial assistance for developers to reduce the cost of construction. PMAY's focus is on "Housing for All," and the scheme supports developers by providing them with capital subsidies, land availability, and tax incentives for constructing homes under the affordable housing category.

- **Interest Subsidies**: Interest subsidy schemes, such as those under PMAY, help developers by reducing the cost of financing for affordable housing projects. By offering lower interest rates on loans, the government makes it easier for developers to access affordable capital. The **Credit Linked Subsidy Scheme (CLSS)**, for instance, provides a subsidy on the interest component of home loans for first-time buyers in the affordable housing segment. This creates an ecosystem where developers are more incentivized to build homes within the financial reach of low-income buyers.
- **Tax Incentives**: The government also offers tax incentives, such as **tax deductions** on profits earned from building affordable homes. For instance, under Section 80-IB of the Income Tax Act, developers constructing affordable housing can claim deductions on their profits for a certain period, encouraging them to focus on the development of affordable housing projects. These tax incentives aim to reduce the developers' financial burden and make affordable housing projects more viable.
- **Subsidies for Sustainable Development**: As part of its commitment to sustainability, the Indian government has introduced subsidies and financial incentives for developers incorporating green building practices. Developers constructing **green buildings** or adopting energy-efficient technologies can benefit from various **subsidies** and **incentives** that reduce their upfront costs. These incentives often come in the form of reduced development charges, rebates, or grants for the use of renewable energy, rainwater harvesting, and waste management systems, among others. Such measures not

only support developers in reducing operational costs but also align them with the country's broader environmental goals.

- **Subsidies for Infrastructure Development**: Infrastructure plays a pivotal role in the success of real estate projects. The government provides various subsidies to developers focusing on improving urban infrastructure, especially in emerging cities and tier-II cities. Developers engaged in urban renewal projects or building infrastructure like roads, water supply, and sewage treatment may be eligible for **subsidies** and **grants** to offset part of the costs involved in such projects. This is particularly relevant for developers working in public-private partnerships (PPP) or projects under the **Smart Cities Mission**, which aims to create efficient, sustainable urban spaces.
- **Public-Private Partnership (PPP) Incentives**: In the case of **PPP projects**, the government may provide various financial incentives to developers, such as land grants, partial funding, and tax exemptions. These projects, particularly in the housing and infrastructure sectors, benefit from a combination of public funding and private expertise, which allows developers to take on large-scale projects with a reduced financial risk. Incentives may also include subsidies for project completion within specific timelines, thus ensuring that critical infrastructure projects are delivered on schedule.

Challenges and Concerns: While grants and subsidies provide crucial financial support, developers often face challenges in availing these benefits. One key issue is the complex application and approval process, which can delay project timelines. Additionally, the scope of subsidies and grants may be limited to specific regions or project types, meaning developers in non-priority areas may not benefit as much. Furthermore, the eligibility criteria for various government schemes can sometimes be stringent, limiting access for smaller developers or projects with less financial backing.

4. Due Diligence for a Real Estate Project

Due diligence is a critical step in real estate transactions, whether for purchasing land or buildings or undertaking development projects. This meticulous process helps developers, buyers, and lenders identify potential risks and assess a project's feasibility. By ensuring compliance with legal, financial, and technical standards, due diligence provides the foundation for making informed decisions and mitigating future disputes.

Importance and Purpose of Due Diligence

Due diligence in real estate serves multiple purposes, including:

1. **Risk Mitigation:** Identifying potential risks before they escalate into major issues.
2. **Informed Decision-Making:** Empowering buyers and lenders with accurate and verified data.
3. **Legal Compliance:** Ensuring property ownership, usage rights, and transaction terms adhere to applicable laws.
4. **Financial Assurance:** Validating the property's profitability and financial viability.
5. **Environmental Awareness:** Assessing environmental factors that may impact the property.
6. **Market Insights:** Understanding market trends and demand to evaluate investment potential.

Types of Due Diligence in Real Estate

1. Market Due Diligence

- Focus: Evaluate the market's potential where the property is located.
- Objective: Identify thriving markets with high growth potential for tenant rents and property prices.
- Example: Selecting an emerging urban locality over a saturated metro hub due to better ROI prospects.

2. Financial Due Diligence

- Focus: Assessing the property's current and projected cash flow.
- Objective: Calculate fair market value and estimate investment returns.
- Activities: Review of income statements, operating expenses, debt obligations, and financial projections.

3. Legal Due Diligence

- Focus: Examining ownership titles, encumbrances, and compliance with land use regulations.
- Objective: Ensure a clear and transferable title with no legal disputes.
- Importance: Especially critical in India due to complex personal laws affecting property inheritance and ownership.

4. Physical Due Diligence

- Focus: Inspecting the property to assess its condition and structural integrity.

- Objective: Verify safety, adherence to standards, and absence of encroachments.
- Example: Ensuring no contamination or environmental hazards are present on-site.

Key Components of Due Diligence

1. Ownership and Title Verification

- Confirm how the property was acquired: sale, gift, will, or lease.
- Ensure that the title deed and historical ownership records are clear and marketable.

2. Encumbrance Check

- Obtain a Non-Encumbrance Certificate (NEC) to verify that the property is free of mortgages, liens, or legal disputes.
- For corporate-owned properties, inspect CHG-1 forms filed with the Registrar of Companies.

3. Zoning and Land Use Compliance

- Ensure that the property complies with local zoning laws and is approved for its intended use (e.g., residential, commercial, agricultural).

4. Government Approvals and Authorizations

- Verify the necessary permits, including:

  i. Building and industrial permissions.

  ii. Environmental clearances.

  iii. Tax payments and insurance policies.

5. Development and Acquisition Risks

- Confirm the legality of ongoing or completed construction as per state and local regulations.
- Ensure the property is not part of government acquisition procedures.

6. Technical Due Diligence (TDD)

- Assessments include:

  i. Structural stability of buildings.

  ii. Soil testing for greenfield lands.

  iii. Inspection of utilities like water, power, and sewage systems.

- **For Existing Buildings:** Examine architectural, civil, mechanical, and electrical systems for defects and compliance.
- **For Greenfield Projects:** Evaluate the land's environmental suitability and feasibility of development.

7. Financial Analysis and CIBIL Check

- Review the financial health of the developer or seller, including their CIBIL score and outstanding liabilities.
- Analyse cash flow, debt servicing capacity, and valuation reports.

8. Publication and Notices

- Publish ownership claims in local newspapers to prevent disputes arising from unregistered transactions.

Due Diligence Checklists

1. Pre-Purchase Checklist

- Legal verification of titles, deeds, and encumbrances.
- Review of sale and conveyance agreements.
- Validation of regulatory approvals (e.g., completion and occupancy certificates).
- Assessment of physical site conditions and amenities.

2. During Construction Checklist

- Pre-construction documentation of the site's natural and structural features.
- Documentation of underground utilities, slab layouts, and progress photographs.

3. Post-Completion Checklist

- Detailed as-built documentation, including utility and structural maps.
- Handoff of technical data to facilities management teams.
- Use of virtual walkthroughs for marketing and pre-sales.

What is the Due Diligence Period in Real Estate?

The due diligence period is a specified time during which buyers and developers evaluate all aspects of a property before finalizing the transaction.

Typical Timeline

1. **Initial Property Review:** 1–2 weeks.
2. **Physical Inspection:** 1–2 weeks.
3. **Title and Legal Review:** 2–3 weeks.

4. **Financial Analysis:** 2–3 weeks.
5. **Environmental Assessments:** 3–4 weeks.
6. **Market Analysis:** 1–2 weeks.
7. **Review of Findings:** 1–2 weeks.

Technical Due Diligence for Real Estate Projects

Technical Due Diligence (TDD) is a specialized process conducted to assess the technical, structural, and operational aspects of a property or land. It provides critical insights into the current condition, compliance, and future maintenance needs of an asset. TDD is essential in evaluating investment risks, ensuring compliance with local regulations, and aligning the property's features with the intended use.

Why Technical Due Diligence is Crucial

1. **Risk Mitigation:** Identifies structural deficiencies, non-compliance with codes, and other risks that could escalate costs or delay projects.
2. **Investment Clarity:** Helps investors understand the property's true condition, enabling better negotiation of purchase prices or lease terms.
3. **Compliance Assurance:** Ensures that the property adheres to building codes, environmental laws, and other local regulations.
4. **Operational Efficiency:** Evaluates whether the property can sustain its intended use without frequent and costly repairs.

Components of Technical Due Diligence

For Existing Buildings:

1. **Document Collection and Review:** Ownership documents, blueprints, structural drawings, and previous inspection reports.
2. **Architectural and External Works:** Inspection of building facades, roofing, and outdoor structures to ensure durability and safety.
3. **Civil and Structural Assessment:** Evaluation of load-bearing capacity, foundation strength, and structural integrity.
4. **Mechanical and Electrical Systems:** Assessment of HVAC systems, plumbing, fire safety systems, and power supply networks for functionality and compliance.
5. **Environmental Evaluation:** Examination of air quality, water drainage systems, and proximity to protected ecological zones.
6. **CAPEX (Capital Expenditure) Cost Estimation:** Forecasting costs for repairs, upgrades, or future maintenance.
7. **Support During Renovation or Repair:** Providing technical guidance and supervision during improvement phases.

For Greenfield Projects:

1. **Land Suitability:** Evaluation of soil stability, flood risks, and geographical factors affecting development.
2. **Topographical Surveys and Soil Tests:** Detailed mapping and testing to confirm the land's viability for construction.
3. **Utility Infrastructure Assessment:** Analysis of existing infrastructure like water supply, power lines, and sewage systems.

4. **Preliminary Design Review:** Creation of initial structural and layout plans aligned with zoning and development guidelines.
5. **Environmental and Location Impact:** Assessment of the location's environmental impact on the property and vice versa.
6. **Cost and Feasibility Studies:** Drafting master plans and calculating the financial viability of the project.

TDD Process and Checklist

Steps to Conduct TDD:

1. **Inspection and Analysis:** Thorough on-site inspection of the property by a team of experts, including architects, engineers, and environmental specialists.
2. **Document Review:** Verification of ownership documents, regulatory approvals, and structural blueprints.
3. **Detailed Reporting:** Compilation of observations into a structured report, highlighting deficiencies, risks, and required actions.
4. **Risk Mitigation Strategies:** Recommendations for resolving identified issues and improving property conditions.

Specific Areas of Focus:

- **Equipment and Systems:** Compatibility and adequacy of on-site machinery and systems for the intended use.
- **Utilities:** Evaluation of energy, water, and waste management systems for efficiency and compliance.
- **Environmental Conditions:** Ensuring the property's surroundings meet local standards and contribute to operational sustainability.

Importance of TDD for Investors

1. **Price Negotiation:** Armed with TDD findings, investors can renegotiate pricing or demand seller-provided remedies.
2. **Avoiding Financial Losses:** Identifying potential repair or maintenance costs upfront prevents unexpected expenses.
3. **Risk Sharing:** Detailed insights allow parties to agree on shared liabilities or responsibilities in contracts.

Checklist for TDD Outcomes

For Completed Projects:

- Compliance with zoning and building laws.
- Operational readiness of mechanical, electrical, and structural systems.
- Final as-built documentation for management and handover.

For Ongoing Projects:

- Updated valuation reports.
- Progress tracking of construction stages.
- Assessment of delays and their financial implications.

For Greenfield Projects:

- Verified soil, topography, and environmental reports.
- Preliminary design approvals.
- Cost estimation for development and infrastructure requirements.

Integrating TDD with Construction Finance

Technical Due Diligence is deeply intertwined with construction finance, ensuring that funding is allocated to viable and compliant projects. Lenders often require detailed TDD reports to assess project risks and decide on loan disbursements.

During Loan Approvals: TDD ensures the project is technically sound and aligned with market demand.

During Construction: Monitoring technical progress and identifying discrepancies or risks.

Post-Completion: Confirming compliance and operational readiness for property sale or lease.

Chapter 6

Construction and Redevelopment

---

1. Construction Finance

Construction Finance Overview

Construction finance is a specialised form of funding dedicated to supporting the development of real estate projects, encompassing both residential and commercial endeavours. This type of financing, commonly called project finance, is crucial for real estate developers, allowing them to bridge funding gaps during the construction phase. It focuses on the projected cash flows generated by the project rather than the financial health of the project sponsors.

In India, real estate is a rapidly growing sector, and both banking and non-banking financial institutions offer construction loans under their project finance departments. Builders or companies engaged in real estate development can avail of these loans to finance their projects. Construction loans are generally secured by the project's assets and are often structured as non-recourse loans, meaning repayment is primarily sourced from the project's cash flows.

Key Features of Project Finance:

- Long-term financing based on future cash flows.
- Secured by project assets, including revenue-producing contracts.
- Lenders often acquire a lien on project assets to assume control if loan terms are not met.

Organizations like CFPL (Construction Finance Private Limited) specialize in arranging project finance for builders and developers. They leverage decades of trust and expertise to deliver tailored financing solutions that maximize the economic value of real estate projects.

Features and Benefits of Construction Finance

Construction finance offers several advantages tailored to meet the unique needs of real estate developers. These features and benefits make it a preferred choice for funding real estate projects:

1. **No Private Investor Required:** Developers can avoid dependence on private investors, reducing the dilution of project control.
2. **Competitive Interest Rates:** Construction loans typically offer better interest rates compared to other funding options, making them cost-effective.
3. **Financial Support:** Provides the necessary capital to ensure smooth project execution without interruptions.

4. **No Extra Collateral Required:** Many lenders offer construction finance without demanding additional collateral beyond the project assets.

The Construction Finance Process

The process for availing of construction finance involves several critical steps to ensure proper evaluation and compliance:

1. **Preparation of a Project Report:** A detailed report outlining the project's scope, feasibility, and expected outcomes.
2. **Company Profile Submission:** Providing a comprehensive overview of the developer's business background and achievements.
3. **Valuation and Legal Report:** Conducting assessments to determine the project's value and legal soundness.
4. **Evaluation Report on Standard Format:** Lenders evaluate the project against specific criteria.
5. **Projection Analysis:** Assessing the developer's past and future financial projections.
6. **Credit History Check:** Reviewing the developer's creditworthiness based on their financial history.
7. **Documentation:** Submission of all required documents for verification and loan processing.
8. **Personal Discussion:** An in-depth discussion with the developer to clarify queries and finalize terms.

Eligibility Criteria for Construction Finance

To qualify for construction finance, applicants must meet certain eligibility requirements set by lending institutions. These criteria ensure that the loan is granted to reliable and capable developers:

1. **Residency and Age:**
   - Must be an Indian resident.
   - Applicant should be above 21 years at the start of the loan and below 65 years at loan maturity.
2. **Professional Experience:** The applicant should have experience as a builder, having completed at least three projects or a minimum constructed area of 100,000 sq. ft.

Required Documents for Construction Finance

The documentation process for construction finance is categorized into **property documents** and **financial documents.**

Property Documents:

1. Detailed project report.
2. Evaluation report in the prescribed format.
3. Legal and technical verification documents.
4. Company profile and past project details.
5. Property ownership and related legal documents.

Financial Documents:

1. Complete financial statements for the past three years (firm level).
2. Individual financial records for the past three years (Directors/Partners/Proprietors).
3. Bank statements for one year (firm and individual accounts).
4. Copies of all existing loan sanction letters.
5. Firm's KYC (registration certificates or licenses).
6. Individual KYC (Directors/Partners/Proprietors).

7. Directors' and auditors' reports for private limited companies.
8. Memorandum and Articles of Association (MOA/AOA).
9. Shareholding patterns on company letterhead.
10. Annual return filings with ROC.
11. Recent photographs.
12. Processing fee cheque.

Types of Projects Eligible for Construction Finance

Lending institutions assess various project types to determine eligibility for construction finance. The following categories outline the kinds of projects that can receive funding:

1. **Vacant Land Projects:**
   - Land must be owned by the firm or promoter.
   - Development agreements with landowners are required.
2. **SRA Projects (Slum Rehabilitation Authority):**
   - If the land is privately owned by the developer, the saleable portion of the construction costs can be financed.
   - A commencement certificate (CC) for the saleable portion is mandatory.
3. **Redevelopment Projects:**
   - In redevelopment projects, only the saleable portion of the construction cost can be financed.
   - A commencement certificate for the saleable area is essential for funding approval.

Process for Availing Construction Finance

The process for obtaining construction finance involves several stages, ensuring compliance and thorough evaluation by the lender:

- **Project Report Preparation:** The developer must submit a project report as per the lender's format, detailing project viability and financial projections.
- **Evaluation of the Project:** A comprehensive evaluation of the project is conducted, including its scope, potential revenue, and risks.
- **Builder/Developer Profile Submission:** Detailed information about the developer's background, experience, and past projects is reviewed.
- **Documentation:** Submission of all property-related and financial documents for verification.
- **Property Valuation:** Independent valuation of the property ensures alignment with market conditions.
- **Personal Discussion:** A direct discussion between the lender and the developer to clarify expectations and address concerns.
- **Loan Sanctioning:** Approval of the loan based on a complete review of the submitted information and evaluations.
- **Disbursement:** Funds are released in phases (slab-wise) depending on project progress.

Note: The process and specific checks, such as residence and office verification or CIBIL score assessments, may vary across lending institutions.

Lender Analysis: Factors Influencing Lending Decisions

When lenders evaluate developers for construction finance, they focus on key performance indicators, track records, and the project's financial viability. Below are critical considerations:

1. Project Success and Quality:

- Timely completion and adherence to the budget of past projects.
- High construction quality and design standards, supported by awards or certifications.
- Profitable financial outcomes from previous projects, reflected in financial statements.

2. Market Conditions:

- Evaluation of market trends during project execution.
- Impact of economic and real estate trends on project demand and success.

3. Risk Management:

- Developer's strategies for addressing challenges, such as delays or cost overruns.
- Contingency plans to mitigate potential risks.

4. Stakeholder Relationships:

- Strong relationships with contractors, suppliers, and the local community.
- Positive associations often lead to smoother project execution and improved reputation.

5. Compliance and Regulatory Record:

- Consistent adherence to legal and regulatory requirements.
- Absence of legal disputes or issues related to previous projects.

6. Innovation and Adaptability:

- Use of sustainable practices and modern construction technologies.
- Ability to adapt project strategies to changing market demands.

7. Customer Satisfaction:

- Feedback from buyers or occupants of completed projects.
- A high satisfaction rate indicates commitment to quality and reliability.

8. Project Diversity and Long-Term Vision:

- Portfolio diversity across sectors, such as residential and commercial properties.
- A strong pipeline of future projects demonstrates sustainability and growth potential.

Cost and Means of Finance Analysis

Cost Breakdown of a Project:

Construction finance analysis involves evaluating the total project cost, segmented as follows:

- **Land Cost:** Acquisition and related expenses.
- **Development Cost:** Construction, labour, and material costs.

- **Stamp Duty and Registration:** Legal and procedural expenses for property registration.
- **Approval Costs:** Charges for obtaining necessary permits and licenses.
- **Construction Cost:** Detailed estimates of building expenses.
- **Marketing and Administrative Costs:** Expenses for project promotion and administrative overheads.

Means of Finance:

To ensure project viability, lenders evaluate the sources of funding:

- **Promoter Contribution:** Equity injection by the developer, reflecting commitment and confidence in the project.
- **Bank/FI Loans:** Debt financing with terms, including interest rates and repayment schedules.
- **Customer Advances:** Pre-sales revenue contributing to project funding.

Key Financial Metrics:

- **Debt-to-Equity Ratio:** Evaluates the balance between borrowed funds and equity.
- **Debt Service Coverage Ratio (DSCR):** Indicates the project's ability to meet debt obligations.
- **Free Cash Flow (FCFF):** The cash available after deducting costs, ensuring debt service capability.

Debt Profile Analysis

Analysing a developer's debt profile is a crucial step for lenders to assess financial health, risk exposure, and repayment capacity. Below are the key components of a debt profile review:

1. Total Debt Outstanding:

- The total debt obligations, including short-term and long-term liabilities, are reviewed.

2. Debt Structure:

- Types of loans (bank loans, bonds, commercial papers).
- Terms such as interest rates, maturity dates, and covenants.

3. Interest Rate Analysis:

- Evaluation of fixed vs. variable interest rates.
- Potential impact of interest rate fluctuations on repayment.

4. Maturity Profile:

- Assessment of debt repayment schedules to avoid large obligations maturing in a short period.

5. Debt Service Coverage Ratio (DSCR):

- The ratio of operating income to debt obligations.
- A healthy DSCR ensures that debt payments can be met.

6. Covenants and Restrictions:

- Financial or operational covenants included in debt agreements.
- Developer's compliance history with these covenants.

7. Collateral and Security:

- Assets provided as security for loans.
- Value and adequacy of collateral in mitigating lender risk.

8. Refinancing Risk:

- Evaluating the ability to refinance or repay maturing debt.

9. Credit Ratings and Default History:

- Developer's credit rating and history of defaults or restructuring.
- Insights into the financial stability and reputation of the borrower.

Land Bank Details

A developer's land bank is a critical indicator of future development potential and financial strength. Lenders examine the following aspects:

1. Land Ownership and Strategy:

- Whether the land is owned outright, acquired through joint ventures, or under development agreements.
- Geographic diversity and strategic location of land parcels.

2. Size and Composition:

- Total land area, zoning classifications, and potential uses.
- Feasibility of development, considering regulations and infrastructure availability.

3. Market Demand Alignment:

- Compatibility of the land bank with current and future real estate market trends.

4. Environmental and Legal Considerations:

- Compliance with environmental laws and absence of disputes or encumbrances.
- Verification of titles to ensure legal clarity.

5. Land Valuation:

- Current market value vs. book value of land parcels.
- Assessment of appreciation potential and carrying costs.

Ongoing Projects: Key Documentation and Metrics

1. Basic Project Information

- **Project Name:** Name of the ongoing development.
- **RERA Registration Number:** Mandatory for all ongoing projects under RERA compliance.
- **Type of Project:** Classification as residential, commercial, or mixed-use.
- **Ownership Details:** Whether the project is on owned land, redevelopment, or SRA (Slum Rehabilitation Authority).

2. Financial Details

- **Total Saleable Area:** Area available for sale in square feet.
- **Landowner's Share vs. Developer's Share:** Split of ownership.
- **Configuration of Units:** Types of units (e.g., 1 BHK, 2 BHK).
- **Pricing and Revenue:**

  i. Total expected sales value.

  ii. Sales value of sold area.

  iii. Revenue from unsold inventory.

  iv. Balance receivable from already sold units.

3. Construction and Approval Stages

- **Project Timeline:**

  i. Date of commencement and expected completion.

  ii. Monthly progress tracking.

- **Approval Status:**

  i. IOD (Intimation of Disapproval).

  ii. CC (Commencement Certificate) status.

  iii. Other relevant approvals.

- **Construction Stage:**

  i. Detailed updates on foundation, slabs, and finishing work.

4. Sales and Customer Data

- **Sold and Unsold Details:**

  i. Total units sold and their configuration.

  ii. Remaining unsold inventory and pricing strategy.

- **Customer Information:**

  i. Name, contact, and agreements of buyers.

  ii. Payment schedules and outstanding dues.

- **Financing Source:**

  i. Home loan details of buyers and the financing institutions involved.

5. Financial Commitments and Existing Loans

- **Existing Loan Details:**

  i. Name of lending bank/financial institution.

  ii. Loan amount, disbursed funds, and outstanding debt.

- **Debt Service Obligations:**

  i. Current repayment schedules and future liabilities.

6. Detailed Flat Allocation List (Sold-Unsold Breakdown)

- **Flat-Wise Data:**

  i. Wing, flat number, floor, and carpet area (as per RERA).

  ii. Saleable area, allotment status, and date of agreement.

- **Payment Information:**

  i. Total agreement amount, received payments, and balance due.

Ongoing Project Analysis

Key Factors in Ongoing Projects:

1. **Project Type:**
   - Residential or commercial projects, as loan terms differ significantly between the two.
2. **Project Configuration:**
   - Evaluation of target market (luxury vs. affordable housing).
   - Appropriateness of project design for the location and audience.

3. **Approval Status:**
   - Verification of necessary permits like IOD (Intimation of Disapproval) and CC (Commencement Certificate).
   - Ensuring construction aligns with regulatory requirements.
4. **Sales and Revenue Analysis:**
   - Expected and actual sales values, comparing per-square-foot rates with market averages.
   - Monitoring sales velocity to assess project demand and performance.
5. **Timeline and Progress:**
   - Comparison of construction stages with projected completion dates.
   - Timely execution demonstrates efficiency and reliability.

Importance of Sales MIS:

- Tracks saleable, sold, and unsold units.
- Provides insights into customer payment schedules, unit pricing, and financial tie-ups with banks.

Completed Project Analysis

Lenders assess completed projects to evaluate a developer's track record, experience, and capability to execute large-scale real estate projects. Here are the primary considerations:

1. Total Construction Area:

- Total area developed across all projects.
- Many financial institutions have thresholds, such as a minimum of 200,000 sq. ft., to qualify for loans.

2. Project Timelines:

- Average time taken to complete projects.
- Consistency in timely project delivery indicates operational efficiency.

3. Developer's Role:

- Confirmation of projects constructed directly by the developer and not just as a contractor.

4. Location and Market Reach:

- Locations of completed projects help determine the developer's presence and market penetration.

5. Historical Gaps in Activity:

- Significant gaps between projects may lead to loan rejections. Developers who stay active in the market are preferred, as they are more likely to stay updated on regulatory and industry standards.

Upcoming Project Analysis

The pipeline of upcoming projects reflects a developer's growth trajectory and potential for revenue generation. Lenders evaluate the following:

1. Project Pipeline:

- Number and scale of upcoming projects.
- Diversity in project types, such as residential, commercial, or mixed-use developments.

2. Approval Status:

- Status of regulatory approvals like RERA registration and local clearances.

3. Financial Planning:

- Assessment of how upcoming projects will be funded.
- Availability of equity, customer advances, or construction finance for these projects.

4. Execution Capability:

- Developer's ability to manage multiple projects simultaneously without financial or operational strain.

Profitability and Free Cash Flow Analysis

Lenders rely on profitability and cash flow metrics to determine a developer's ability to repay loans and sustain operations.

1. Profitability Assessment:

- **Formula:** Profit = Total Revenue – Total Project Cost
- Profit margins indicate the financial health of projects.

2. Free Cash Flow (FCFF):

- **Formula:** FCFF = Amount Receivable from Sold Units + Value of Unsold Inventory – Cost Yet to be Incurred
- Free cash flow shows surplus funds available after meeting project costs, which lenders use to determine loan eligibility.

3. Debt-to-Equity Ratio:

- The ratio between borrowed funds and equity contribution.
- Lenders prefer a 2:1 debt-to-equity ratio for healthy financial leverage.

4. Contingency Planning:

- Adequate contingency funds ensure resilience against unexpected challenges.

Funding Strategies During Construction

Real estate developers employ various funding strategies to sustain cash flow during the construction phase. These strategies are crucial for maintaining operations and ensuring timely project completion.

Sales as a Funding Strategy

Sales play a pivotal role in funding construction activities, as revenue from unit sales directly contributes to project financing.

1. Importance of Sales:

- Real estate products are high-value assets with appreciation potential.
- Successful sales strategies ensure steady cash flow, reducing dependency on loans.

2. Payment Plans:

Developers offer various payment plans to attract buyers and ensure financial inflow:

Construction-Linked Payment Plan (CLP):

Buyers pay instalments based on the completion of construction milestones.

For example:

- 10% at booking.
- 10% at foundation completion.
- Subsequent instalments at each slab completion.
- Balance on possession.

Subvention Scheme:

A tripartite agreement between the buyer, developer, and bank, where:

- Buyers pay 5–20% upfront.
- Banks finance the remaining amount directly to the developer in instalments.
- Developers bear the interest cost until project completion.

Advantages:

- Buyers avoid initial EMIs.
- Developers secure significant funding upfront.
- Lenders have regulated disbursement schedules.

Risks:

- Hidden costs may inflate property prices.
- Default by developers can impact buyers' credit reputation.

Barter as a Funding Strategy

Barter transactions involve exchanging goods or services instead of monetary payments, commonly used in construction.

1. Application in Real Estate:

- Developers provide units or spaces to contractors or suppliers in return for their services or materials.
- Ratios typically range from 60:40 to 100% barter agreements.

2. Benefits:

- Reduces immediate cash outflow for developers.

- Offers higher value to contractors as the exchange is often above cash-equivalent rates.

3. Challenges:

- Limited applicability, dependent on contractor/vendor agreement.
- Risks of overvaluation of the exchanged assets.

Stages of Construction and Cost Monitoring

The construction phase of a project is broken into multiple stages, each requiring careful financial oversight to ensure timely progress and cost control. Effective monitoring at every stage ensures the project remains on budget and schedule.

1. Stages of Construction

a. Foundation and Structural Work:

- Includes excavation, laying the foundation, and constructing the framework.
- Significant funds are allocated at this stage for materials and labour.

b. Plinth and Slab Construction:

- Construction progresses through individual floors, often slab by slab.
- Each milestone triggers payments under Construction-Linked Payment Plans (CLP).

c. Masonry and Internal Works:

- Installation of walls, windows, doors, and internal fittings such as plumbing and wiring.

d. Finishing Work:

- Final touches, including painting, tiling, and interior finishing.

e. Possession Stage:

- Final delivery of units to buyers. Any remaining dues, such as the last 5% in payment plans, are collected at this stage.

2. Cost Monitoring and Allocation

a. Budget Allocation:

- Project costs are allocated to different stages and monitored to ensure adherence to the budget.
- Overruns are addressed through contingency funds.

b. Progress-Based Disbursement:

- Lenders release funds slab-wise or based on progress reports, reducing the risk of fund misuse.

c. Variance Analysis:

- Compares actual spending with projected budgets to identify deviations early.

d. Contingency Planning:

- A contingency reserve is maintained to handle unforeseen costs like material price escalations or delays.

Role of Sales MIS in Monitoring Performance

Sales Management Information System (MIS) provides critical insights into project performance, ensuring transparency and accountability.

1. Key Metrics Tracked by Sales MIS:

- **Saleable Area:** The total area available for sale, split between the developer and landowner.
- **Unit Classification:** Tracks allotted, registered, and unsold units.
- **Agreement Dates and Values:** Helps analyse average per-square-foot pricing.
- **Receipts and Dues:** Monitors customer payments against the construction stage.

2. Lender Perspective on Sales MIS:

- Cross-verifies pricing strategies with nearby projects to ensure market competitiveness.
- Assesses sales velocity, indicating demand and project performance.

Profitability and Financial Viability

Profitability and free cash flow are crucial metrics for lenders to determine the financial health of a project and its developer. These metrics provide insights into the project's ability to sustain operations, service debt, and generate returns.

1. Profitability Assessment

- **Formula:** Profit = Total Revenue – Total Project Cost
- Profit margins indicate the project's success and the developer's efficiency in managing costs while achieving desired revenues.

Key Considerations:

- **Revenue Generation:** Factors like pricing strategies and sales velocity directly impact revenue.

- **Cost Management:** Effective budget control and reduction of overruns enhance profitability.

2. Free Cash Flow (FCFF)

- **Formula:** FCFF = Amount Receivable from Sold Units + Value of Unsold Inventory – Cost Yet to be Incurred
- Free cash flow represents the liquidity available after covering project expenses, which is critical for loan repayment.

Significance for Lenders:

- Determines the developer's ability to meet debt obligations.
- Acts as a benchmark for loan amounts; for example, lenders may provide loans at a 2:1 free cash flow-to-loan ratio.

Land Bank Analysis

A developer's land bank represents the foundation for future growth and a significant asset for financial leverage. Lenders analyse the land bank to assess its potential and value.

1. Composition and Value:

- Total land area held, categorized by zoning and developmental potential.
- Valuation of land based on market trends and future growth prospects.

2. Strategic Location:

- Well-located parcels align with market demand, boosting profitability potential.

3. Legal and Environmental Compliance:

- Clear titles and environmental compliance reduce risks during development.

4. Carrying Costs:

- Includes taxes, maintenance, and other holding expenses, impacting profitability.

Upcoming Project Pipeline

The pipeline of upcoming projects reflects a developer's growth potential and long-term sustainability. Lenders evaluate it to understand future revenue streams and operational capacity.

Key Metrics for Upcoming Projects:

- **Number of Projects:** Indicates the developer's ambition and scale of operations.
- **Approval Status:** Ensures compliance with RERA and other local regulations.
- **Planned Revenue:** Projects the financial impact of future developments.
- **Execution Capability:** Assesses the developer's ability to handle simultaneous projects.

Impact on Loan Decisions: A strong pipeline reassures lenders of continuous revenue generation and demonstrates the developer's forward-looking strategy and market positioning.

2. Redevelopment Projects and self-redevelopment

Redevelopment

Redevelopment involves demolishing old buildings and replacing them with modern structures to enhance utility, value, and living standards. This process is common in urban areas where space is limited, and demand for housing and commercial spaces is high. The goal is to utilize land effectively while ensuring improved infrastructure and amenities for residents. Redevelopment projects often focus on increasing Floor Space Index (FSI), modernizing amenities, and adhering to urban planning standards.

Self-Redevelopment

Overview:

Self-redevelopment is a process where housing societies independently undertake redevelopment without involving external developers. This approach is gaining traction in cities like Mumbai due to delays and disputes in traditional redevelopment models. In self-redevelopment, societies fully control the project, from planning to execution, ensuring transparency and accountability.

Self-Redevelopment Finance

According to Anarock's research, as of May 2022, approximately 1,28,870 housing units were stalled in Mumbai. This has understandably led to apprehension among those planning redevelopment projects. Consequently, there has been a renewed focus on self-redevelopment as a viable solution.

Initially, the Reserve Bank of India (RBI) permitted only the Mumbai District Cooperative Bank to fund self-redevelopment projects. However, a recent notification has expanded this provision, allowing societies to borrow from housing finance companies (HFCs) as well.

MHADA, designated as the supervising authority, alongside the state government, has been actively promoting the self-redevelopment model. This initiative has encouraged banks and financial institutions to recognize its potential. With the introduction of single-window approval systems, obtaining all necessary permissions for self-redevelopment has become more streamlined.

Under this model, lenders can finance up to 95% of the project cost at a competitive simple interest rate of 12.5% annually, according to the latest reports. The remaining funds must be arranged by society members. The repayment tenure typically extends up to seven years for projects costing up to ₹50 crores. Notably, for a project to proceed under self-redevelopment, unanimous consent from all building members is essential.

Management companies

To effectively manage finances during self-redevelopment, housing societies should establish a committee comprising individuals with expertise in finance and the redevelopment process. As the society assumes the role of the developer, it holds responsibility for overseeing project funds. Given the dynamic nature of cash flows, it is crucial to plan financial requirements at the outset of the project and continuously monitor and adjust them as the project progresses. To bridge gaps in expertise, numerous consultancy and management firms have emerged, offering professional guidance and assistance throughout the redevelopment process. These firms provide services such as securing necessary approvals, organizing finances, and overseeing project execution. By engaging such experts for a fee, societies can reduce dependency on developers and maintain control over the redevelopment process. In cities like Mumbai, consultancy firms are increasingly becoming essential for housing societies. These firms manage every aspect of the redevelopment process, from financial planning and manpower coordination to government approvals and the sale of additional flats generated through increased FSI or TDR. Their comprehensive services enable societies to execute projects in alignment with their specific needs and objectives while ensuring regulatory compliance and smooth operations.

Financing Self-Redevelopment

1. **Internal Contributions:**

   Societies use existing funds or raise additional contributions from members to initiate the project.

2. **Bank Loans:**

   The Reserve Bank of India (RBI) has allowed cooperative housing societies to borrow from housing finance companies (HFCs). For instance, the Mumbai District Cooperative Bank finances up to 95% of project costs at an interest rate of 12.5%, with subsidies reducing it to 8.5%. Loan repayment terms are seven years, with a two-year moratorium.

3. **Non-Banking Financial Companies (NBFCs):**

   NBFCs provide loans against mortgage assets, funding the project during initial stages up to the IOD (Intimation of

Disapproval) clearance. They play a crucial role in financing projects where societies face cash flow challenges.

4. **Pre-Sale of Flats:**

   Societies can sell new flats constructed under increased FSI at competitive rates, raising funds for construction.

5. **Investors and Deposits:**

   Societies invite members, friends, or external investors to contribute to the project, offering lucrative returns (10-12% annually).

6. **Barter System:**

   Contractors are compensated with rights to sell a portion of the flats equivalent to their construction costs.

Paperwork for Self-Redevelopment

Documents Required for Funding:

- Ownership and plot documents.
- Feasibility reports.
- Architect\u2019s plans and permissions from local authorities (e.g., BMC).

Financial institutions may request additional documentation for due diligence. An Intimation of Disapproval (IOD) is often a prerequisite for loan approval.

List of Approvals Required for Construction

S. No.	Approval	Concerned Agency	Remarks
1	Ownership Certificate/ Extract	Revenue Department	Required by Development Authority/ Town & Country Planning Department/ Municipal Corporation for other approvals.
2	Non-Encumbrance Certificate	Revenue Department	Ensures the property is free from legal dues; required by other agencies for approvals.
3	Change in Land Use (CLU) Approval/ Non-Agriculture (NA) Permission	Development Authority/ Revenue Department/ Municipal Corporation	Converts agricultural land to residential, commercial, or industrial use; notified by State Ministry of Urban Development.
4	Airport Clearance (if applicable)	Airport Authority of India	Height clearance required if the project lies within 20 km of airstrips or funnel areas.

S. No.	Approval	Concerned Agency	Remarks
5	CRZ (Coastal Regulatory Zone) Clearance	Coastal Zone Management Authority	Required if the project is within 500 meters of the coastline.
6	Layout & Building Plan Approval	Development Authority/ Municipal Corporation	Includes structural plans for buildings and other structures.
7	Development/ Construction License	Development Authority/ Town & Country Planning Department	Requires site inspection by the authority.
8	Demarcation/ Zoning Plan Approval	Town & Country Planning Department	Required in some states as a separate approval, in addition to the layout plan.
9	Environment Clearance	Ministry of Environment & Forests/ SEIAA/ State Pollution Control Board	Required for projects exceeding a land area of 125 acres or a built-up area of 20,000 sq. meters.

S. No.	Approval	Concerned Agency	Remarks
10	NOC for Tree Cutting	Municipal Corporation/ Forest Department	Proposal for tree felling and replantation must be submitted.
11	NOC for Drainage & Sewerage	Municipal Corporation	Required before the start of construction.
12	Electrical Scheme Approval	Development Authority/ Municipal Corporation/ Electricity Distribution Company	Electrical layout and plan must be submitted.
13	NOC for Traffic & Coordination	Municipal Corporation/ Traffic Police Department	Required if the proposal disrupts general traffic movement or circulation temporarily or permanently.
14	Fire Fighting Scheme Approval	Fire Department	Applicable for buildings exceeding the minimum height specified by the city's municipal corporation.

S. No.	Approval	Concerned Agency	Remarks
15	Ancient Monument Approval (if applicable)	Archaeological Survey of India	Necessary if the project is within 300 meters of a monument protected under the Ancient Monuments Act.
16	Consent to Establish & Operate (DG Sets & STP)	Pollution Control Board	Required for the installation of DG sets and sewage treatment plants.
17	Borewell Registration Certificate	Central Ground Water Authority	Required for extracting groundwater through energized means, as per the Environment Protection Act.
18	Excavation/ Mining Approval	Development Authority/ Municipal Corporation	Approved drawings and plans must be submitted.

S. No.	Approval	Concerned Agency	Remarks
19	Internal Infrastructure Layout & Common Facilities Approval	Municipal Corporation/ Utility Provider	Layout drawings and plans for water, electricity, sewerage, etc., must be submitted for approval.
20	Road Access Plan Approval	NHAI/ PWD/ State Road Development Agency	Approval required as per the PWD Act to ensure seamless access to the project site from adjoining roads.
21	Lift Escalator Installation Approval	PWD/ CPWD	AMC copy and test report must be submitted.
22	Sanction of Electrical Load and Substation/ Transformer Approval	Electricity Distribution Company	Electrical plans and test reports must accompany the application.
23	Registration of Principal Employer	Labour Department	Mandatory under the Contract Labour Act in many states.

S. No.	Approval	Concerned Agency	Remarks
24	Registration with Building Construction Workers Welfare Board	District Labour Officer	Required under the Contract Labour Act in many states.
25	Site Office Approval	Development Authority/ Town & Country Planning Department	Affidavit must state that the site office will be dismantled after project completion.
26	Hoarding Approval	NHAI/ PWD/ Land Owning Agency	Required for displaying project hoardings.
27	Intimation of Disapproval (IoD)/ Commencement Certificate	Development Authority/ Municipal Corporation	Issued after submission of all required applications, plans, and NOCs.
28	Completion Certificate (CC)	Development Authority/ Municipal Corporation	Issued after confirming that the building complies with sanctioned plans; a provisional occupancy certificate is also issued.

S. No.	Approval	Concerned Agency	Remarks
29	Permanent Power Connection	Electricity Distribution Company	Applied for after receiving the completion certificate and provisional occupancy certificate.
30	Permanent Water Connection	Municipal Corporation/ State Water Board	Required to ensure water supply for the property.
31	Permanent Sewerage Connection	Municipal Corporation/ State Water Board	Necessary for proper waste management systems.
32	Registration of Residents' Welfare Association (RWA)	Revenue Department	Mandatory before occupancy certificate is issued.
33	Occupancy Certificate (OC)	Development Authority/ Municipal Corporation	Confirms that the property is fit for occupation.

The list above represents a general overview of the approvals typically required for construction projects. However, it is important to note that some states may impose additional requirements to be fulfilled.

For homebuyers or real estate investors, scrutinizing every approval in such a comprehensive list may not be feasible. Instead, it is advisable to focus on four critical approvals that provide assurance of the project's legitimacy and compliance:

- **Ownership Certificate / Extract**

  Verifies the developer's ownership of the land. Prospective buyers can also cross-check land records online for additional due diligence.

- **Change in Land Use (CLU) Approval**

  Confirms the conversion of agricultural land into residential, commercial, or industrial use, as permitted by the relevant authorities.

- **Layout & Building Plan Approval**

  Ensures that the proposed layout and building design have been sanctioned by the development authority or municipal corporation prior to the commencement of construction.

- **Commencement Certificate**

  Confirms that the builder has obtained all necessary approvals and No Objection Certificates (NOCs) required to begin construction.

It is crucial to avoid investing in any project where these key approvals are incomplete or missing. If a builder evades questions or attempts to deflect inquiries regarding these approvals, it may indicate non-compliance and an effort to prematurely market the project. Additionally, upon project completion, buyers should ensure that the builder has obtained both the **Completion Certificate** and the **Occupancy Certificate** to affirm that the property adheres to approved plans and is fit for habitation.

Benefits of Self-Redevelopment

Control and Transparency: Societies manage the entire process, ensuring cost efficiency and accountability.

Financial Gains: Additional flats constructed under increased FSI can be sold to generate revenue.

Faster Approvals: Single-window clearance systems simplify obtaining permissions.

Time-Bound Execution: Societies can avoid delays associated with traditional redevelopment models.

Reduced Risk: Avoids dependency on developers, reducing the likelihood of disputes or financial issues.

Success Stories

1. **Jin Prem Housing Society (Charkop, Mumbai):**

   Completed a 14-story self-redevelopment project with 53 flats (705 sq. ft. each) funded entirely by 28 society members without external loans.

2. **New Tilak Nagar Riddhi Siddhi CHS (Chembur):**

   Located on a 998 sq. mtr plot owned by MHADA, this society\u2019s redevelopment process is underway.

3. **Mukund Employees\u2019 CHS (Ghatkopar West):**

   A 43-member society on a 2,068 sq. mtr plot currently undertaking self-redevelopment.

4. **Om Rameshwar CHS (Borivali East):**

   Self-redevelopment is ongoing, initiated by 26 members.

5. **Chitra Cooperative Housing Society (Chembur):**

   A 15-story project with 12 completed floors; members received flats double their previous size, with 32 additional flats for sale.

6. **Purvarang Society (Mulund):**

   A 23-story project under construction, with members receiving flats double the size of their old units. Extra flats will be sold in the open market.

Other notable projects include Malad Apartment CHSL, Shalimar Society, and Kshitij Society.

3. Joint Ventures (JVs) and Joint Development Agreements (JDAs)

Joint Ventures (JVs)

A **Joint Venture (JV)** is a strategic alliance between two or more parties that combine their resources to undertake a real estate project. Typically, these ventures are formed between developers and landowners or among large national developers and regional players. Each partner shares responsibilities, profits, and risks based on the terms of the agreement.

PROs

A joint venture allows each side to benefit from the resources of the other(s) without investing a lot of money. Once the joint venture is completed, each company can maintain its own name and resume normal business operations. Joint ventures also provide the advantage of risk sharing.

CONs

Joint venture agreements frequently restrict partner companies' outside activity while the project is under process. Exclusivity agreements or non-compete agreements that affect present ties with vendors or other business contacts may be needed of each company engaging in a joint venture. Unless a distinct business entity is established for the joint venture, the contract under which joint ventures are formed may subject each company to the liability inherent in a partnership. Furthermore, while joint venture partners share ownership, work activities, and resource allocation are not necessarily distributed equitably.

Financing in JVs

In JV financing, **equity contributions** from each partner fund the initial stages of the project, such as land acquisition or construction. Often, these contributions are leveraged to secure **debt financing** from banks or private lenders. The project's **revenue-sharing structure** is crucial in financing arrangements, as it dictates how profits and expenses are allocated between the partners. **Debt financing** typically comes from construction loans, institutional funding, or even private equity, depending on the project's scope. The JV structure, by distributing risks and rewards, allows developers to lower their capital investment while sharing operational responsibilities.

Funding Challenges

Joint ventures can face challenges like **lack of clarity** in terms of profit-sharing, resulting in disputes over the distribution of resources or ownership stakes. Additionally, financing institutions are cautious if one or more partners lack creditworthiness, or if the **terms of the joint venture** are not clearly outlined. Regulatory approvals and transparency issues could also delay financing, making it critical to have clear agreements and legal backing.

Joint Development Agreements (JDAs)

Overview

In a **Joint Development Agreement (JDA)**, the landowner offers the right to develop their land in exchange for a share of the revenue or a built-up area. This model is especially popular in urban areas where developers prefer not to purchase land directly but instead acquire the right to develop it.

PROS

A JDA provides various advantages to both parties as long as they continue to work together. Communication and paperwork are critical in this situation. The builder's and landlord's rights and responsibilities must be clearly defined in the JDA's terms and conditions. Because getting into such agreements implies that you're in it for the long haul, clear and constant communication between the contracting parties is essential. If any complications occur in relation to these two components, the entire agreement may quickly become sour and, as a result, stuck.

CONS

- Long-term commitment is required in real estate. Disagreements and arguments can damage the process's longevity.
- Many new rules governing joint developments may emerge over the lengthy process, posing a risk to the agreement.

- Everything the two sides have agreed to on paper may not turn out to be as good as they had hoped.
- Joint development agreements are complicated by nature, and they should not be taken into lightly or without legal advice.

Financing in JDAs

The developer, after securing the land rights through the JDA, approaches financial institutions for **construction finance**. The initial payments made to the landowner, if any, may be funded using short-term loans or equity infusions. **Revenue models** like pre-sales or leasing the developer's share of the project can be used to fund construction costs. Often, lenders may provide funds based on the **FSI (Floor Space Index)** and expected return on investments.

Funding Challenges

Since JDAs typically involve a **non-ownership structure** of land, financing institutions might be cautious in offering loans without clear agreements on land rights and regulatory approvals. The **revenue-sharing model** is another point of concern, as both parties need to adhere to it strictly. Legal disputes or a lack of clarity on **built-up area division** can complicate financing processes.

4. Development Management (DM) Model

Overview

The **Development Management (DM)** model is a collaboration where large, reputed developers manage the construction and development process for smaller regional players or landowners. Under this model, the big developers bring in their expertise, project management skills, and brand reputation, while local developers or landowners provide the land and share in the profits.

Financing in DM Models

DM financing generally involves **external funding** from banks, NBFCs, or private equity, as the developer manages the project on behalf of the landowner. **Revenue share agreements** are common, where the developer is compensated through **management fees** or a share of the project's profits. For local landowners, financing may come from **equity infusions**, **construction loans**, or **pre-sales** agreements. The involvement of larger developers reduces the perceived risk, making it easier to secure institutional funding.

Funding Benefits

The DM model is **asset-light**, meaning the large developer doesn't need to invest in land acquisition, and therefore, has lower upfront costs. **Institutional lenders** view the involvement of reputable developers as a **risk mitigator**, which makes financing more accessible. Furthermore, local developers benefit from the access to skilled resources and brand association, which aids in project quality and timely delivery.

Funding Challenges

Financing can still face challenges from **lack of local expertise**, unclear **revenue-sharing arrangements**, and **delays in approvals**. A mismatch in expectations between large developers and local landowners may disrupt the smooth flow of funds.

5. Types of projects and their means of obtaining Funds

(i) Greenfield Projects

Greenfield projects refer to developments built on previously undeveloped land. These are typically large-scale projects, such as residential complexes, commercial developments, or mixed-use townships, constructed in newly acquired or unutilized areas.

Funding Requirements:

Greenfield projects are capital-intensive, requiring significant upfront investment for land acquisition, infrastructure development, and construction. Financing for such projects is sought through a combination of equity, debt, and sometimes government incentives.

Sources of Finance:

- **Equity Financing**: Developers may seek **private equity investments** from fund houses, institutional investors, or high-net-worth individuals (HNIs). The investors expect a share in the profits from the completed project.
- **Bank Loans/Construction Finance**: Banks typically offer **term loans, construction loans**, and **working capital finance**. Lenders evaluate the viability of the project based on the developer's reputation, project size, and expected cash flows.
- **Real Estate Investment Trusts (REITs)**: Large developers may raise capital by listing part of their completed projects as part of a **REIT** structure, enabling fund houses and retail investors to invest in income-generating real estate assets.

- **Mezzanine Financing**: This is a hybrid financing structure between debt and equity, where developers may raise funds through **mezzanine loans** from venture capitalists or private equity firms. These funds are riskier and come with higher returns, typically secured by a stake in the project.

Example:

Developers like **DLF** and **Lodha** have undertaken Greenfield projects on the outskirts of major cities like Delhi and Mumbai, where funding is sourced from a blend of **developer equity**, **bank loans**, and **private equity funds**.

(ii) Brownfield Projects

Brownfield projects involve the redevelopment or renovation of existing properties. This can include transforming old factories into residential complexes, repurposing warehouses into office spaces, or modernizing commercial properties.

Funding Requirements:

Brownfield projects are generally less capital-intensive than Greenfield developments because the land is already available. However, substantial funding is still required for construction, renovations, legal clearances, and sometimes demolition.

Sources of Finance:

- **Debt Financing**: Since Brownfield projects are often located in established areas with existing infrastructure, they are less risky for lenders. **Banks** provide construction loans, often backed by the income generated from the existing property or its future rental value.

- **Private Equity**: **Private equity funds** are often interested in Brownfield projects because they promise quicker returns due to the existing infrastructure. These funds provide capital in exchange for equity in the project.
- **Structured Finance**: Developers may enter into **structured finance deals**, such as **sale and leaseback** agreements or **asset-backed financing**, where the property itself serves as collateral for the loan.
- **Partnerships and Joint Ventures (JVs)**: Developers may enter into **joint ventures** with landowners or other stakeholders, sharing profits from the project. Financing in this case may come from equity investors or **development finance institutions**.

Example:

A company like **Phoenix Mills** redeveloping old mill land into commercial properties in Mumbai would raise finance through **debt instruments**, **private equity**, and potentially through **sale and leaseback** arrangements.

(iii) Slum Redevelopment Authority (SRA) Projects

SRA projects are specific to the redevelopment of slum areas in Indian cities. In these projects, developers work with the **Slum Redevelopment Authority (SRA)** to build housing for slum dwellers, while the developer also retains a portion of the property for sale or commercial use.

Funding Requirements:

The cost structure is somewhat different for SRA projects due to government involvement, as the developer needs to account for both the construction of slum dwellings and the cost of acquiring land or giving **Built-Up Area (BUA)** to the landowners.

Sources of Finance:

- **Equity & Debt**: The financing for SRA projects often involves **equity investment** by the developer, followed by **bank loans** for construction and development. The loans are typically **project-specific loans** based on the income generated from the sale of the **developed portion** of the property.
- **Government Funding**: In certain cases, state and central government subsidies and grants may be provided to incentivize the construction of affordable housing and slum redevelopment projects.
- **Joint Ventures with Landowners**: Developers may enter into **joint ventures** with the landowners, where the landowners contribute land while the developers bring in capital for construction, and profits are shared accordingly.

Example:

Developers like **Shapoorji Pallonji** or **Kalpataru** have successfully executed **SRA redevelopment** projects in Mumbai. The funding typically comes through a blend of **developer equity**, **loans**, and **government schemes**.

(iv) Affordable Housing Projects (PMAY)

These are residential projects aimed at providing affordable housing for the lower-income population, often supported by government schemes like the **Pradhan Mantri Awas Yojana (PMAY)**.

Funding Requirements:

Affordable housing projects require less capital due to the lower cost of construction per unit, but they still require financing for land acquisition, development, and construction.

Sources of Finance:

- **Government Subsidies and Funding**: The **PMAY scheme** offers **subsidized loans** and **interest rate subsidies** for developers working on affordable housing projects. Developers can also access funds through **National Housing Bank (NHB)** for such projects.
- **Low-Cost Debt Financing**: **Banks** may provide lower interest loans for affordable housing projects, as the government guarantees some level of financial support for such developments.
- **Private Equity**: Private investors can also participate in affordable housing projects, seeking lower but steady returns over a longer period.

Example:

Developers like **Mahindra Lifespace** and **Oberoi Realty** have successfully secured funding for affordable housing projects under PMAY by partnering with the government and using **low-cost financing options**.

(v) Commercial Real Estate Projects

Commercial real estate projects involve the development of office buildings, retail spaces, industrial parks, and hotels. These projects are designed for business use and are typically more capital-intensive.

Funding Requirements:

Commercial projects have high upfront costs due to land acquisition, design, construction, and regulatory approvals.

Sources of Finance:

- **Bank Loans & Term Loans**: Commercial real estate developers rely on **term loans** from commercial banks, which may offer higher loan amounts due to the lucrative rental or sales income expected from commercial spaces.
- **Private Equity**: Private equity or **real estate investment funds** play a significant role in funding large commercial developments. These funds expect returns through rental yields or capital appreciation.
- **REITs**: **REITs** (Real Estate Investment Trusts) are increasingly being used by developers to raise capital for large commercial projects. These provide a way for developers to access funds while maintaining ownership of the property.

Example:

Phoenix Mills and **Brigade Group** have funded large-scale commercial developments in metropolitan areas through **bank loans**, **private equity**, and **REITs**.

(vi) Mixed-Use Development Projects

Mixed-use developments combine residential, commercial, and recreational spaces into one integrated development. These projects aim to provide a self-sustained living experience and are often part of large-scale townships.

Funding Requirements:

Mixed-use developments require diverse financing options due to the multiple components involved (residential, commercial, and amenities).

Sources of Finance:

- **Equity Financing**: Developers often raise capital from **private equity investors** who are willing to take a long-term stake in both the residential and commercial aspects of the project.
- **Bank Loans**: A combination of **construction loans** and **term loans** from banks is common, with the loan amount tied to the projected income from both residential and commercial units.
- **Structured Finance**: **Structured finance products** such as **mezzanine finance** or **collateralized loans** may be used to bridge funding gaps in large-scale mixed-use projects.

Example:

Developers like **Lodha Group** and **Godrej Properties** use a combination of **equity financing, bank loans**, and **REITs** to fund mixed-use developments like **Palava City** and **Godrej Garden City**.

Chapter 7

Developer Premiums

Floor Space Index (FSI)

Understanding real estate terms is of utmost importance when navigating the complex world of property transactions. It empowers individuals to make informed decisions, negotiate effectively, and avoid costly mistakes. Among the key terms in real estate, one that holds significant relevance is Floor Space Index (FSI), also known as Floor Area Ratio (FAR).

FSI represents the ratio of a building's total floor area to the size of the land on which it stands. It plays a crucial role in checking the density and development potential of a property. FSI can be further categorized into Premium FSI, which allows for additional construction rights upon payment of a fee. FSI calculation defines the maximum allowed construction on a given site. Thereby ensuring efficient land utilization while adhering to zoning regulations and infrastructure capacity.

Understanding FSI and its implications is essential for investors, developers, and buyers. This knowledge helps evaluate the potential of a property, comply with building regulations, and make informed decisions.

What is FSI?

The Floor Space Index (FSI) is a critical concept in real estate. FSI determines the maximum amount of construction allowed on a plot of land relative to its size. It is calculated by dividing the total floor area of a building by the area of the plot.

Understanding FSI is important because it helps regulate urban development. By setting limits on FSI, authorities can control the density of buildings, manage infrastructure capacities, and maintain the overall balance of an area. FSI ensures that buildings are not overcrowded and that there is enough open space for amenities and public use.

For example, if a plot has an FSI of 2, it means that the total floor area of the building cannot exceed twice the size of the plot. This limit prevents excessive construction and helps maintain a harmonious urban environment.

FSI is a crucial factor in urban planning and zoning regulations. It ensures that buildings are constructed in accordance with the available infrastructure and resources such as water, electricity, and transportation networks. By adhering to FSI guidelines, developers can contribute to sustainable and well-planned urban development.

How to Perform FSI Calculation?

Performing FSI calculation involves a straightforward FSI formula. By performing the FSI calculation, property owners, developers, and authorities can assess the maximum allowable construction on a particular plot of land.

To calculate FSI, divide the total covered area of all floors by the plot area. Here's an example to illustrate the process:

Let's say you have a plot of land with an area of 500 square metres, and the total covered area of all floors in the building is 750 square metres. To calculate the FSI, divide 750 (total covered area) by 500 (plot area):

FSI = Total Covered Area / Plot Area FSI = 750 square metres / 500 square metres FSI = 1.5

In this example, the FSI is determined to be 1.5. It means that the total floor area of the building should not exceed 1.5 times the size of the plot. If the FSI allowed by local regulations is 2, then the building can be expanded further to utilize the available FSI.

Types of development premiums

(i) Premium FSI

Premium FSI is an additional concept related to Floor Space Index (FSI) in real estate. It allows developers to exceed the standard FSI limits upon payment of a fee. Premium FSI provides an opportunity for increased construction rights beyond the regular FSI. Thereby, enabling developers to construct larger buildings and maximize the potential of a property.

The importance of premium FSI lies in its contribution to urban development and revenue generation. By offering premium FSI, authorities can generate additional funds that can be invested in infrastructure development, public amenities, or other projects. It also provides developers with flexibility in their construction plans.

For developers, premium FSI can be a valuable tool for increasing the revenue potential of a project. It enables them to construct more floors or expand the building's footprint, thus including more units or commercial spaces. This can lead to higher rental income or property values, thereby improving returns on investment.

How to Perform Premiums FSI Calculation?

Performing Premium FSI calculation involves a similar process to regular FSI calculation but with the additional factor of the premium fee. Here's an example to illustrate the calculation:

Let's assume you have a plot of land with an FSI limit of 2, and the plot area is 500 square metres. If you want to exceed the regular FSI limit and utilize premium FSI, you need to pay a premium fee. Suppose the premium fee is Rs. 10,000 per square meter.

First, calculate the regular FSI by multiplying the plot area by the FSI limit:

Regular FSI = Plot Area x FSI Limit

Regular FSI = 500 square metres x 2

Regular FSI = 1000 square metres

Next, determine the premium FSI by subtracting the regular FSI from the desired total FSI:

Premium FSI = Total FSI - Regular FSI

Suppose you want a total FSI of 1500 square metres. The premium FSI would be:

Premium FSI = 1500 square metres - 1000 square metres

Premium FSI = 500 square metres

Finally, calculate the premium fee by multiplying the premium FSI by the premium fee rate:

Premium Fee = Premium FSI x Premium Fee Rate

Premium Fee = 500 square metres x Rs. 10,000 per square meter

Premium Fee = Rs. 50, 00,000.

Hence, by paying the premium fee, you can utilize an additional 500 square metres of construction beyond the regular FSI limit.

Factors Affecting FSI

The Floor Space Index (FSI) is influenced by various factors that determine the maximum permissible construction on a plot of land. Here are five key factors affecting FSI:

Zoning Rules

Zoning rules set by local authorities play a crucial role in deciding FSI. These rules define permissible land use, building setbacks, height restrictions, and FSI limits for specific zones or areas. The FSI calculation is influenced by the zoning rules applicable to a particular plot.

Infrastructure Capacity

FSI also affects the availability and capacity of infrastructure systems. This includes systems like water supply, sewage, transportation networks, and public amenities. Authorities consider the infrastructure's ability to support additional construction. Then it determines the impact on the nearby area when deciding the FSI limits.

Environmental Considerations

Environmental Considerations: Environmental factors, such as open space requirements, ecological areas, and environmental impact studies, can affect FSI. Authorities may impose restrictions or allocate additional FSI to ensure environmental sustainability and protect natural resources.

Road Width and Setbacks

The width of the adjacent roads and building setbacks can influence FSI. Narrower roads or larger setbacks may result in reduced FSI limits. This would ensure proper circulation, parking, and access to the building, while wider roads may allow for higher FSI.

Building Type and Function

The type of building and its function can impact FSI. Residential, commercial, industrial, and institutional buildings may have different FSI limits based on local rules. For example, higher FSI may be allowed for commercial buildings as compared to residential premises.

Benefits of understanding FSI

Understanding FSI, or Floor Space Index, offers numerous benefits for individuals involved in real estate.

Here are some key advantages:

Property Evaluation

Knowledge of FSI allows potential buyers and investors to evaluate the development potential of a property accurately. By understanding the maximum allowable construction and density, they can assess the feasibility of their plans. Thus, they are in a better position to calculate and estimate potential returns on investment and make informed decisions.

Compliance with Regulations

FSI helps developers and property owners comply with local zoning and building regulations. By understanding the FSI rules, they can design and construct buildings that adhere to the prescribed guidelines. Thereby, ensuring legal compliance and avoiding penalties.

Optimal Land Utilization

Floor Space Index enables efficient land utilization by controlling the density of buildings. It ensures that available land is used wisely, balancing the needs of development with open spaces, amenities, and infrastructure requirements. Understanding FSI helps in maximizing the utilization of available space.

Sustainable Development

FSI plays a vital role in promoting sustainable urban development. By regulating building density and size, FSI ensures that urban areas are developed in a manner that supports infrastructure capacity and conserves resources. It helps maintain a balance between population growth and available amenities.

Informed Decision-making

Understanding FSI empowers all stakeholders to make informed decisions regarding property investments and construction plans. It allows them to understand the limitations and opportunities associated with a particular property.

(ii) TDR (Transferable Development Rights)

What is TDR?

TDR is a mechanism that allows developers or property owners to transfer unused Floor Space Index (FSI) from one property to another. This system is typically used in urban areas where density control is necessary. TDRs are especially useful when land is in a high-demand zone, allowing for more efficient land use in such areas. Instead of utilizing the FSI on one property, owners can sell or transfer this FSI to another plot, usually within the same city or region.

How TDR Works:

If a property has unused FSI (the maximum construction rights permitted), that FSI can be sold or transferred to a different location where higher density is permitted or needed.

Typically, these transfers occur from lower-density areas (like green zones or conservation areas) to higher-density urban areas where construction is permissible.

Benefits of TDR:

- **Promotes sustainable development**: TDR encourages the preservation of open spaces, heritage areas, or low-density zones while allowing increased construction in urbanized areas.
- **Revenue generation**: Municipalities can earn revenue by facilitating the transfer of development rights.
- **Urban renewal**: TDR facilitates rejuvenating urban areas by increasing development potential in targeted zones.

(iii) Land Premium

What is Land Premium?

A land premium is charged by municipal authorities when there is a change in land use, such as rezoning land from industrial to residential. The premium compensates the local body for the loss of revenue or the change in the land's development potential.

When is it Applied?

When the development of land is permitted for a higher-density or more profitable use (e.g., changing agricultural or industrial land to residential or commercial).

Purpose of Land Premium:

To recover development rights: The premium is paid to the authorities in exchange for new rights granted by changing the land use.

Infrastructure financing: The collected premiums can fund public infrastructure in the area.

(iv) Parking Premium

What is Parking Premium?

In areas where developers are required to provide parking as per local zoning and planning norms, a parking premium allows them to pay fees to exceed or bypass certain parking requirements. This is especially useful in urban areas with limited space.

How it Works:

If the developer cannot provide the required number of parking spaces on-site due to limited land area, they can pay a premium to the local authorities for additional parking permissions or access to shared parking facilities nearby.

Purpose:

To meet parking requirements: It helps developers meet the stringent parking norms while maximizing construction potential.

Urban planning flexibility: Allows more efficient land use in congested urban centres.

(v) Water and Sewerage Premium

What is Water and Sewerage Premium?

Developers may need to pay a water and sewerage premium when the local infrastructure, like water supply or sewage systems, is inadequate or overburdened. This premium helps fund improvements to the existing infrastructure to accommodate new development.

When is it Used?

When a proposed development will strain existing water or sewage infrastructure, developers pay this premium to finance necessary upgrades.

Purpose:

Infrastructure support: It ensures that the development doesn't overwhelm essential public services.

Cost sharing: It spreads the costs of upgrading water and sewerage systems across new developments.

(vi) Open Space Premium

What is Open Space Premium?

Open Space Premium allows developers to bypass or reduce the amount of open space required for their projects. This premium is paid to local authorities in exchange for permission to use more land for construction instead of dedicating it to public open space, parks, or recreational facilities.

How it Works:

Developers may be required to provide a certain percentage of their land for public open space. If they want to reduce this percentage, they can pay a premium to the local authorities.

Purpose:

To balance development needs with public amenities: The premium ensures that even if developers reduce open spaces, funds are available to enhance public areas nearby.

Encouraging development: It provides flexibility to developers while ensuring public amenities are maintained.

(vii) Tree Cutting Premium

What is Tree Cutting Premium?

This premium is charged when developers cut down trees for construction. The payment is intended to compensate for the environmental loss caused by the removal of trees and to fund replantation or environmental preservation efforts.

How it Works:

Developers must pay a fee for each tree removed, which is used to fund tree planting programs or other environmental restoration activities.

Purpose:

Mitigate environmental impact: Ensures the sustainability of urban development by funding replantation or other eco-friendly initiatives.

Environmental responsibility: Helps preserve green cover and biodiversity in cities.

(viii) Cooperative Housing Societies Premium

What is Cooperative Housing Societies Premium?

This premium is paid by developers to cooperative housing societies in redevelopment projects. It's typically used when developers seek to relocate society members to allow for increased construction rights or higher FSI.

How it Works:

Developers may offer a premium to cooperative societies in exchange for the society's consent to demolish and redevelop the property with higher FSI.

Purpose:

Incentivize redevelopment: Helps encourage cooperation between developers and society members for smooth redevelopment.

Provide better living standards: Ensures that the society members are compensated or relocated to better homes.

(ix) Heritage Premium

What is Heritage Premium?

Heritage Premium is paid by developers when constructing in or near designated heritage areas, where stringent regulations limit development. The premium compensates for the costs of preserving historical landmarks and architectural features.

How it Works:

Developers are required to preserve or integrate heritage elements within their project, and the premium helps offset the costs of this compliance.

Purpose:

Preserve cultural heritage: Ensures the protection and preservation of historical structures or areas.

Facilitates development: Allows developers to modify their plans to fit within heritage preservation guidelines while compensating for the additional efforts required.

(x) Floor Usage Premium

What is Floor Usage Premium?

Floor Usage Premium is applicable when developers wish to change the designated use of floors within a building (e.g., converting residential floors into commercial space). This premium is paid to local authorities for approval of the change.

How it Works:

Developers pay a premium for converting the function of floors (e.g., changing a residential building into a commercial one) in compliance with zoning regulations.

Purpose:

Flexible usage: Encourages mixed-use developments or adaptation of buildings to market demand.

Regulate land use: Ensures that such changes comply with zoning laws and urban planning norms.

(xi) Height Premium

What is Height Premium?

This premium is charged when a developer wishes to exceed the prescribed building height limits. It allows developers to construct taller buildings than normally permitted by paying a fee to local authorities.

How it Works:

Developers can request a height concession by paying a premium, enabling taller structures where the local zoning laws might typically restrict building heights.

Purpose:

Maximize construction potential: Allows developers to utilize vertical space in urban areas.

Urban densification: Facilitates the creation of high-rise buildings in areas with limited land availability.

(xii) Setback Premium

What is Setback Premium?

Setback Premium allows developers to reduce the distance that a building must be set back from the plot boundary. This enables developers to maximize the usable area of their plot, increasing the overall built-up area.

How it Works:

Developers may request a reduction in the setback requirement by paying a premium.

Purpose:

Increase usable space: Helps developers maximize the available space for construction.

Provide flexibility: Allows for more efficient design and utilization of the land.

(xiii) Slum Redevelopment Premium

What is Slum Redevelopment Premium?

This premium is given to developers for the additional FSI or other benefits they receive when involved in slum redevelopment projects. These projects aim to upgrade slum dwellings, providing better living conditions while also allowing developers to construct higher buildings in the area.

How it Works:

Developers are granted additional construction rights (FSI) in exchange for rehabilitating slum dwellers and improving their living conditions.

Purpose:

Upgrade slum areas: Helps in improving housing conditions for low-income communities.

Encourage private sector participation: Provides developers with incentives to participate in social housing projects.

(xiv) Rehabilitation Premium

What is Rehabilitation Premium?

Rehabilitation Premium is paid when residents or tenants are temporarily or permanently relocated during redevelopment projects. Developers pay this premium to ensure displaced residents are provided with alternate housing or financial compensation.

How it Works:

Developers may need to relocate residents as part of redevelopment, and the premium helps cover costs like temporary accommodations, rehabilitation, or relocation expenses.

Purpose:

Support displaced residents: Ensures that redevelopment does not harm existing communities.

Maintain social harmony: Helps in providing fair compensation and relocation options for residents impacted by redevelopment.

(xv) Energy Efficiency Premium

What is Energy Efficiency Premium?

The Energy Efficiency Premium is a reward for developers who incorporate energy-saving features into their buildings, such as solar panels, rainwater harvesting systems, or energy-efficient building materials. Developers may be given additional FSI or other benefits in return for sustainable practices.

How it Works:

Developers who adopt green technologies and eco-friendly practices are eligible to pay a lower premium or earn incentives like additional FSI.

Purpose:

Encourage sustainability: Helps promote green building practices and environmental responsibility.

Reduce development costs: Incentivizes developers to adopt sustainable and cost-effective building practices.

(xvi) Funding of BMC Premiums

In order to maintain basic civic amenities and provide infrastructural facilities in the city, property tax acts as one of the principal sources of revenue for the Urban Local Bodies (ULB's). As per the census report, Mumbai is the home of about 20.5 million people. Brihanmumbai Municipal Corporation (BMC) is responsible for collecting property tax in Mumbai.

BMC, which is also known as Municipal Corporation of Greater Mumbai (MCGM), is India's richest municipal corporation. As per the last budget presented by the BMC, the share of property tax stands around 22% of the total revenue.

Unlike other municipal corporations of the country, BMC calculates property tax based on the market value of the property. BMC uses Capital Value System to calculate property tax which in turn based on the market value.

BMC Property Tax Computation Method

Apart from the market value, BMC also considers other factors like carpet area, use factor, age factor, floor and occupancy factors.

The formula used for the property tax calculation by the BMC is as follows:

Property Tax = Tax Rate * Capital Value

Where: Capital Value = Market Value of the Property (Based on the Ready Reckoner) * Total Carpet Area * Use Factor * Age Factor * Floor Factor * Occupancy Factor

Here, the market value of the property is based on the ready reckoner which is used to calculate the stamp duty by the revenue department. Ready reckoner calculates the market value of the property using the area rates published by the Government of Maharashtra in a book called Annual Statement Rates (ASR).

Use factor is whether the property is residential or non-residential.

Age factor assigns the weight as per the year in which the property was constructed.

Floor factor depends on the floor on which the property is located. Floor factor is inversely proportional to the floor number.

Occupancy factor is dependent on whether the property is self-owned or rented.

You can pay your property tax online at BMC website by furnishing the required details including ward no, zone, locality, carpet area, usage and occupancy type, year of construction and floor type.

Part 6

Finance for Homebuyers

Chapter 1

Home Loan

What is a Home Loan?

A home loan is a secured loan provided to individuals to help them purchase, construct, or renovate a home. The property purchased with the loan acts as collateral for the loan. Home loans offer long repayment periods, typically spanning from 10 to 30 years, and come with relatively low-interest rates compared to unsecured loans. These loans are typically repaid through monthly instalments (EMIs) until the total loan amount, along with interest, is fully paid off. Once the loan is repaid, the borrower gains full ownership of the property.

Types of Home Loans

1. Loans for Land Purchase Many banks offer loans for land purchase, allowing buyers to purchase land for future development or investment. Such loans are often provided at up to 85% of the land's cost, and the buyer can either build a house on it later or hold the land for future value appreciation. This type of loan gives flexibility for future construction, with the plot's cost included in the loan.

2. Home Purchase Loans This is the most common type of home loan and is meant for the purchase of a new or resale home. Typically, these loans cover up to 85% of the property's value. Interest rates for home purchase loans can range from 9.85% to 11.25%, depending on the lender and loan terms. The loan may be available with either fixed or floating interest rates.

3. Loans for Home Construction These loans are specifically for individuals who want to build a house on a plot of land they already own. The loan amount is based on the estimated construction cost, and it can be disbursed either as a lump sum or in stages, as the construction progresses. To qualify, applicants must purchase the plot within one year of taking the loan.

4. Loans for House Expansion or Extension Some banks offer loans for home expansion or renovation, which could include adding a room, balcony, or garage to the existing structure. These loans cater to individuals looking to expand their current living spaces, and some popular examples include HDFC Home Extension loans.

5. Loans for Home Conversion A home conversion loan allows borrowers who already have a home loan to shift their loan to a new property without repaying the previous home loan in full. This is ideal for those who are relocating or upgrading to a better home.

6. Home Improvement Loans Home improvement loans cover repairs, renovations, and the addition of features like a new overhead water tank or electrical work. This type of loan is typically used for enhancing the quality and value of the existing property.

7. Home Loans with Balance Transfer A balance transfer loan allows a borrower to transfer an existing home loan from one lender to another, typically to secure a lower interest rate or better terms. This is a useful option for those looking to reduce their repayment burden by switching to a more favourable lender.

8. Home Loans for Non-Resident Indians (NRIs) NRIs can avail themselves of home loans designed specifically for them, with distinct formalities and application processes. These loans are typically available for purchasing residential properties in India, and many public and private sector banks offer these loans.

9. Bridged Loans Bridged loans are short-term loans that assist homeowners in purchasing a new home before selling their existing one. This type of loan typically provides funding until the old property is sold, and the loan term is usually less than two years.

10. Loans for Stamp Duty Some banks provide loans to cover the stamp duty charges incurred during the property transaction. This type of loan is relatively less common but is useful for buyers who need assistance with the upfront costs involved in purchasing a property.

Advantages of Home Loans

1. Feeling of Accomplishment: Purchasing a home is often one of the most significant financial decisions in an individual's life. It provides not just shelter but also a sense of achievement, as the property typically represents a large part of one's investment portfolio.

2. Capital Appreciation: Over time, real estate has historically appreciated in value, making it one of the most profitable investments. The cost of construction, which constitutes a large portion of a home's price, typically rises by 10-15% annually. Hence, owning a home can serve as a hedge against inflation and offer long-term financial security. As home values increase, the borrower benefits from both the rise in property value and lower interest rates.

3. Tax Advantages:

   - Interest Deduction: Home loans offer significant tax benefits. Under Section 24(b) of the Income Tax Act, homeowners can deduct up to Rs. 1.5 lakh from their taxable income for the interest paid on home loans. If the loan was taken before March 1, 1999, the deduction is limited to Rs. 30,000. Additionally, interest paid during the pre-construction period can be deducted in five equal instalments starting from the year the property is completed or acquired.

   - Principal Repayment Deduction: Under Sections 80C and 80CCE of the Income Tax Act, homeowners can claim a deduction of up to Rs. 1 lakh on the principal repayment of their home loan. This allows borrowers to reduce their taxable income by including home loan principal repayment as part of their investments.

Home Loan Eligibility

The eligibility for a home loan depends on several factors, including the applicant's age, income, employment stability, and credit score. Here are the key eligibility criteria:

- Age: Typically, the applicant should be between 21 to 60 years of age.
- Income: A stable income, whether salaried or self-employed, is required. Lenders assess the applicant's monthly income to determine their repayment capacity.
- Employment Status: Salaried employees, self-employed individuals, and NRIs can apply, provided they meet the specific requirements of the lender.
- Credit Score: A good credit score (usually above 750) enhances the chances of loan approval and may qualify the borrower for lower interest rates.
- Property Valuation: The loan amount is often determined by the property's market value, which will be assessed by the lender's appraisal team.

Home Loan Interest Rates

Home loan interest rates vary across lenders and depend on several factors. The rates are generally either fixed or floating:

- Fixed Interest Rate: The interest rate remains constant throughout the loan tenure.
- Floating Interest Rate: The rate fluctuates with market conditions, typically in line with the lender's benchmark rate.

Interest rates usually range from 8.5% to 11.5%, depending on the lender, the applicant's credit score, and market trends. Some lenders may offer lower rates for specific customer segments (e.g., women borrowers, government employees).

Documents Required for Home Loan

i. Identity Proof:
   - Passport
   - Aadhar Card
   - Voter ID
   - PAN Card

ii. Address Proof:
   - Utility Bills (electricity, water)
   - Rent Agreement
   - Passport
   - Aadhar Card

iii. Income Proof:
   - Salary Slip (Last 3 months)
   - Form 16
   - Income Tax Returns (Last 2 years)
   - Bank Statements (Last 6 months)

iv. Property Documents:
   - Title Deed
   - Sale Agreement
   - Approved Building Plan
   - Encumbrance Certificate

v. Employment Documents (for salaried individuals):
   - Employment Contract
   - Employer's Certificate
   - Payslips (Last 3 months)

vi. Self-Employment Documents (for self-employed individuals):
   - Business Registration Certificate
   - Profit and Loss Statement
   - Balance Sheet
   - Income Tax Returns (Last 3 years)

vii. Photographs:
   - Passport-sized photographs of the applicant(s) and co-applicant(s)

viii. Other Documents:
   - Processing Fee Cheque (if required)
   - Power of Attorney (if applicable)

Home Loan Balance Transfer:

A home loan balance transfer, also known as a loan refinancing, is the process of transferring the outstanding loan amount of an existing home loan from one lender to another. Borrowers typically opt for a balance transfer to benefit from better terms, such as a lower interest rate, improved repayment tenure, or enhanced customer service.

Key Features of a Home Loan Balance Transfer

1. Outstanding Loan Transfer: Only the unpaid portion of the home loan is transferred to the new lender.
2. Better Interest Rates: The primary reason for the transfer is to reduce the interest burden, which can result in lower EMIs (Equated Monthly Instalments).
3. Flexible Terms: The new lender may offer better repayment terms, including longer or shorter tenures.

4. Top-Up Loan: Borrowers may also get the option to avail a top-up loan (an additional loan) for personal or home-related expenses.

Step-by-Step Process

1. **Evaluate Savings:**
   - Calculate the potential savings from a reduced interest rate.
   - Include processing fees, prepayment penalties, and other costs.
   - Ensure the savings outweigh the transfer expenses.
2. **Apply to the New Lender:**
   - Submit an application to the new lender with required documents, such as proof of income, loan repayment track record, and property papers.
   - The new lender will assess the borrower's creditworthiness and the property.
3. **Get a No Objection Certificate (NOC):**
   - Request a NOC and foreclosure letter from the existing lender. This document details the remaining loan amount and confirms the closure of the loan once repayment is made.
4. **Loan Sanction by New Lender:**
   - Once approved, the new lender disburses the outstanding loan amount directly to the existing lender.
5. **Loan Closure with Existing Lender:**
   - The previous loan account is closed, and the property documents held by the old lender are transferred to the new lender.

6. **Begin Repayment with the New Lender:**
   - The borrower starts repaying the loan under the terms agreed with the new lender.

Benefits of Home Loan Balance Transfer

1. Lower Interest Rates: Reduces the overall cost of borrowing.
2. Reduced EMIs: Lower monthly repayments due to decreased interest rates.
3. Top-Up Loan Facility: Additional funds can be availed.
4. Improved Services: Switch to a lender with better customer service or loan management facilities.

Costs Involved

1. Processing Fee: Charged by the new lender for processing the transfer application.
2. Foreclosure Charges: If applicable, some lenders charge fees for closing the loan before the original tenure ends.
3. Legal and Valuation Charges: The new lender may charge fees for property valuation or legal verification.

When to opt for a Balance Transfer?

1. If the current lender's interest rate is significantly higher than market rates.
2. When the borrower has a strong repayment history and credit score, increasing the chances of securing better terms.
3. If the remaining loan tenure is long enough to justify the cost of transfer.

Chapter 2

Second Mortgage Loan

What is a Second Mortgage Loan?

A second mortgage is a lien placed on a property that already has a mortgage. It allows homeowners to borrow against the equity they've built in their property. The funds can be used for various purposes, such as debt consolidation or home improvements. Since the loan is secured by the property, second mortgages often have lower interest rates than unsecured loans or credit cards.

Process of Second Mortgage Loan

To obtain a second mortgage:

1. Assess your home equity. Lenders typically allow borrowing up to 80–90% of the equity.
2. Meet the credit score requirement (usually 620 or higher).
3. Ensure your debt-to-income ratio (DTI) is below 43%.
4. Submit an application and provide necessary documentation (see the full list below).
5. Undergo a property appraisal to determine your home's current market value.

6. Receive approval, sign the agreement, and disbursement begins.

Types of Second Mortgage Loan

1. **Home Equity Loan**
    - Provides a lump sum based on your equity.
    - Requires monthly payments with interest over a set term (5–30 years).
    - Suitable for large, one-time expenses.
2. **Home Equity Line of Credit (HELOC)**
    - Functions like a credit card with a revolving balance.
    - Has a draw period during which you can use and repay funds, followed by a repayment period.
    - Ideal for recurring expenses like tuition or home repairs.

Eligibility for a Second Mortgage Loan

- **Age**: Minimum 21 years.
- **Employment**: Stable salaried or self-employed income.
- **Credit Score**: Minimum 620, though higher scores improve loan terms.
- **DTI Ratio**: Typically, below 43%.
- **Equity Requirement**: At least 20% of the home's value must remain unencumbered after borrowing.

Interest Rates for Second Mortgage Loans

Second mortgage loan interest rates are generally higher than first mortgage rates but lower than unsecured loans like credit cards. Rates depend on factors such as:

- Credit score.
- Loan type (fixed vs. variable).
- Loan-to-value ratio (LTV).

Typical interest rate ranges:

- **Home Equity Loan**: 8–12%.
- **HELOC**: 7.5–10%, with variable rates based on market conditions.

Documents Required for a Second Mortgage Loan

i. **Identity Proof**:
   - Passport, Aadhaar Card, PAN Card, or Voter ID.

ii. **Address Proof:**
   - Utility Bills, Rent Agreement, or Passport.

iii. **Income Proof**:
   - Salaried: Latest 3 months' salary slips and Form 16.
   - Self-Employed: Profit and Loss Statement, Balance Sheet, and IT returns (last 2 years).

iv. **Property Documents**:
   - Original Sale Deed or Title Deed.
   - No-Objection Certificate (NOC) from the first mortgage lender.
   - Latest property tax receipts.

v. **Loan Documents**:
   - First mortgage loan agreement.
   - Bank statements showing EMI payments (last 12 months).

vi. **Other Documents**:

- Passport-sized photographs.
- Cheque for processing fee.

Advantages of Second Mortgage Loan

- **High Loan Amounts**: Borrow up to 90% of your home equity.
- **Lower Interest Rates**: Rates are typically lower than credit cards or personal loans.
- **Flexible Usage**: Funds can be used for any purpose, including education, home renovations, or debt consolidation.

Disadvantages of Second Mortgage Loan

- **Risk of Losing Your Home**: If you default on payments, the lender may foreclose on your property.
- **Additional Debt**: Increases your overall debt obligations.
- **Higher Interest than First Mortgages**: Rates are higher compared to primary mortgage loans.

Chapter 3

Reverse Mortgage loan

What is a Reverse Mortgage Loan?

A reverse mortgage is a loan designed for homeowners aged 62 or older, allowing them to borrow against the equity in their homes. Instead of making monthly payments to the lender, the lender pays the homeowner in fixed monthly payments, a lump sum, or a line of credit. The loan does not require repayment until the borrower sells the home, moves out permanently, or passes away. Federal regulations ensure that the loan amount does not exceed the home's value. Mortgage insurance protects borrowers or their estates from owing more than the home's value.

Types of Reverse Mortgage Loans

1. **Home Equity Conversion Mortgage (HECM)**
    - Federally insured and the most common type of reverse mortgage.
    - Available for properties that meet FHA requirements.
2. **Proprietary Reverse Mortgage**
    - Offered by private lenders.

- Suitable for high-value homes that exceed HECM limits.

3. **Single-Purpose Reverse Mortgage**
   - Limited use for specific expenses, such as property taxes or home repairs.
   - Often provided by local or state government agencies.

Process of Reverse Mortgage Loan

1. **Application**: Select a lender and provide basic personal and property details.
2. **Counselling**: Borrowers must attend mandatory HUD-approved counselling to understand terms and responsibilities.
3. **Home Appraisal**: Determines the market value of the property.
4. **Loan Approval**: After appraisal and document verification, the lender approves the loan.
5. **Payment Disbursement**: Borrowers can choose lump-sum, fixed monthly payments, or a line of credit.

Eligibility for Reverse Mortgage Loans

1. **Age**: Borrowers must be at least 62 years old.
2. **Property Type**:
   - Single-family homes, approved condos, or multi-family homes (up to 4 units with borrower occupying one unit).
   - Excludes cooperative housing and manufactured homes built before 1976.
3. **Equity**: At least 50% equity in the property.

4. **Ownership**: Borrower must either own the property outright or have a low outstanding balance on the primary mortgage.

Sanction of Reverse Mortgage Loans

1. **Loan Amount Calculation:**
   - Based on borrower's age, interest rates, and home equity.
2. **Interest Rates**: Fixed or variable, often between 7–10%.
3. **Documentation**:
   - Proof of identity, income, and property ownership.
   - Appraisal report and property tax receipts.

Default and Foreclosure

Default: Occurs if the borrower fails to:

- Pay property taxes or homeowners insurance.
- Maintain the property in good condition.

Foreclosure:

- Initiated if the borrower violates loan terms or stops living in the property for over 12 months.
- Lender sells the property to recover the loan balance.

Refinancing Reverse Mortgage Loans

Refinancing a reverse mortgage is possible under the following circumstances:

- **Adding a Spouse**: To include a new co-borrower.
- **Equity Increase**: To access additional equity.

- **Interest Rate Reduction**: If lower rates can offset the costs of refinancing.

Is Reverse Mortgage Beneficial?

Reverse mortgages provide financial flexibility for seniors by allowing them to access home equity without selling their homes or making monthly payments. However, they may reduce home equity over time and carry fees such as mortgage insurance premiums and origination costs. Seniors should carefully evaluate their financial needs and consult with advisors before proceeding.

Chapter 4

Loan Against Property

What is a Loan Against Property (LAP)?

A Loan Against Property (LAP) is a type of secured loan where borrowers pledge their property as collateral to secure funds from a financial institution. The pledged property can include residential houses, commercial properties, industrial premises, or land. The loan amount is disbursed based on the property's market value and the borrower's repayment capacity. This type of loan is popular due to its relatively low interest rates compared to unsecured loans like personal loans. Since the property remains mortgaged with the lender until the loan is fully repaid, it provides significant security to the lender. Borrowers can use LAP funds for various purposes, including business expansion, debt consolidation, education, or medical emergencies.

Types of Properties That Can Be Mortgaged Under LAP

LAP is versatile in terms of eligible properties. Here's a breakdown:

- **Residential Properties**: Includes self-occupied or rented properties, such as apartments, flats, and standalone houses.

- **Commercial Properties**: Office spaces, shops, malls, and retail spaces qualify for LAP.
- **Industrial Properties**: Factories, warehouses, and other industrial premises can be used as collateral.
- **Land Parcels**: Vacant or agricultural land owned by the borrower is also eligible for LAP, depending on the lender's policies.

The property must be legally owned by the borrower and free of disputes. Banks and lenders also ensure that the property adheres to local government and zoning regulations before approving the loan.

Key Facts About Loans Against Property

1. **Loan Tenure**: LAP offers flexibility with repayment periods ranging from 2 to 20 years, depending on the lender's policies and the borrower's preferences.
2. **Processing Fee**: Typically, lenders charge 1%-2% of the loan amount as processing fees.
3. **Loan-to-Value Ratio (LTV)**: Borrowers can get loans up to 70% of their property's market value, though some lenders may offer up to 90%.
4. **Tax Benefits**: If the loan amount is used for business purposes, interest paid on the loan qualifies for tax benefits under Section 37(1). If the loan is used for property repairs or construction, tax benefits can be claimed under Section 24(b).
5. **Interest Rates**: Generally, range from 9% to 12% annually.
6. **Usage Restrictions**: LAP cannot be used for speculative investments or activities deemed illegal under the law.

Loan Amount Considerations for LAP

The amount sanctioned under LAP depends on several factors:

- **Market Value of Property**: Lenders assess the current market value through an evaluation conducted by experts. They then offer a percentage (50%-70%) as a loan. Some NBFCs may extend loans up to 75%.
- **Borrower's Profile**: Apart from the property value, lenders evaluate the borrower's financial health, including credit history, repayment capacity, income stability, and obligations.
- **Loan-to-Value Ratio (LTV)**: For instance, if a property is valued at ₹1 crore and the LTV ratio is 70%, the borrower can get ₹70 lakhs as a loan.

Eligibility for LAP

Eligibility criteria vary slightly between salaried and self-employed individuals:

1. **For Salaried Individuals:**
    - **Age**: Between 33 to 58 years.
    - **Employer**: Should be employed in a private, public, or multinational company.
    - **Residency**: Indian residents only.
2. **For Self-Employed Individuals**:
    - **Age**: Between 25 to 70 years.
    - **Income**: Must have a stable and regular income.
    - **Residency**: Must be an Indian resident.

Additional requirements include clean ownership of the property and a good credit score.

LAP Prepayment

Borrowers can prepay their LAP, but the terms depend on the type of interest rate:

- **Floating Interest Rate**: Prepayment can be made without penalties.
- **Fixed Interest Rate**: Prepayment might attract penalties, as specified in the loan agreement.

Loan Tenure: Borrowers can opt for a tenure as short as 2 years or as long as 20 years. Overdraft facilities (LAP-OD) are typically sanctioned for up to 24 months, with the option to extend them based on the lender's discretion.

Differences Between LAP and Home Loan

Although both LAP and home loans involve property, they serve different purposes:

- **Purpose**: LAP allows you to borrow funds using your property as collateral, whereas home loans are specifically for purchasing or constructing properties.
- **Tax Benefits**: LAP offers tax benefits only for business or property-related purposes, while home loans provide deductions for both interest and principal components.
- **Loan Amount**: LAP provides funds up to 70% of the property's value, whereas home loans typically cover 75%-90% of the property's value.
- **Repayment Tenure**: Both offer long repayment terms, but LAP provides greater flexibility for diverse financial needs.

Risks Associated With LAP

LAP comes with certain risks, including:

- **Risk of Losing Property**: If the borrower defaults on repayment, the lender has the right to seize and auction the mortgaged property.
- **Impact on Credit Score**: Defaults result in penalties and negatively affect the borrower's creditworthiness.
- **Limited Tax Benefits**: Salaried individuals cannot claim tax benefits on the principal repayment of LAP.

Sanction and Disbursement of LAP

The sanction process involves:

1. **Document Submission**: Includes proof of income, property ownership documents, and other personal details.
2. **Property Valuation**: Conducted by experts appointed by the lender to determine the market value.
3. **Approval and Disbursement**: Based on the borrower's financial eligibility, the sanctioned amount is disbursed either as a lump sum or in phases.

Default and Foreclosure in LAP

In cases of default, lenders impose penalties and initiate legal proceedings if the borrower repeatedly fails to make payments. **Foreclosure** occurs when the lender seizes and auctions the property to recover dues. After recovering the loan amount, any surplus from the sale is returned to the borrower.

Chapter 5

FRACTIONAL OWNERSHIP

Fractional ownership is an innovative investment model that allows individuals to share ownership of high-value assets like real estate, luxury goods, and artwork. By dividing these assets into smaller, more manageable shares, fractional ownership democratizes access, reduces individual costs, and provides opportunities for diversification. Below, we explore the fundamentals, benefits, challenges, and applications of this ownership structure.

The Basics of Fractional Ownership

Fractional ownership involves dividing an asset into shares that multiple investors can purchase. Each fractional owner holds a proportionate stake, with rights and responsibilities defined by ownership percentage. For instance, in a property divided into ten equal shares, each owner possesses one-tenth of the asset. This structure enables shared ownership, cost distribution, and accessibility to assets otherwise unattainable for individual investors.

Lower Cost of Entry

High-value assets, such as luxury properties, private jets, or rare artwork, are often out of reach for individual buyers. Fractional ownership allows investors to acquire partial shares, significantly reducing the financial entry barrier. For example, instead of buying an entire vacation home, an individual can purchase a share, gaining access to the property without the full financial commitment.

Shared Expenses and Cost Efficiency

Ownership of valuable assets entails ongoing expenses like maintenance, taxes, and insurance. Fractional ownership distributes these costs proportionally among investors, reducing individual financial strain. This collective approach ensures cost efficiency and makes managing high-value assets more accessible.

Diversification: A Strategic Advantage

Fractional ownership allows investors to diversify their portfolios by acquiring shares in multiple assets across various industries and locations. Diversification minimizes risk and enhances potential returns, making it an attractive option for those seeking to optimize their investment strategies without needing significant capital.

Professional Management

Many fractional ownership arrangements include professional management services to handle maintenance, operations, and rental optimization. This relieves owners of day-to-day responsibilities while ensuring the asset is well-maintained and continues to generate value.

Applications of Fractional Ownership

Real Estate:

Fractional ownership is particularly prevalent in real estate. Investors can collectively own residential or commercial properties, sharing the costs and benefits proportionally. This model is especially appealing for high-value properties in prime locations, offering both investment returns and potential rental income.

Luxury Goods:

High-end items like private jets, yachts, luxury cars, and rare artwork are also common in fractional ownership arrangements. Owners share the use and maintenance costs of these assets, making luxury more accessible to a broader audience.

Vacation Properties:

In sought-after destinations, fractional ownership enables individuals to own and enjoy vacation homes for specific periods while generating rental income during non-use. This blend of leisure and investment offers financial and lifestyle benefits.

Commercial Real Estate:

Investors can participate in fractional ownership of income-generating commercial properties, such as office buildings or shopping centres. Rental income is distributed among owners based on their shares, offering a reliable source of returns without the full burden of sole ownership.

Challenges of Fractional Ownership

- Limited Control:

  Shared ownership often requires consensus for major decisions, such as renovations or sales. Disagreements among owners can lead to delays or gridlocks, limiting individual control over the asset.

- Complex Legal Arrangements:

  Fractional ownership agreements are detailed legal documents outlining rights, responsibilities, and rules for decision-making, expense sharing, and dispute resolution. Investors must thoroughly understand these terms to avoid potential conflicts.

- Liquidity Constraints:

  Selling a fractional ownership share can be challenging, as it often requires finding a buyer through private sales. The limited liquidity of shares makes it difficult for investors to quickly access their capital.

- Management Fees:

  While professional management enhances asset performance, it incurs additional costs. These fees can reduce net returns, requiring owners to balance the benefits of professional services against their financial impact.

Chapter 6

PERSONAL LOANS

Personal loans in India are unsecured loans provided by banks and financial institutions that can be utilized for various purposes, including home-related expenses. Although they are not specifically designed for purchasing property, homebuyers often use personal loans for expenses like down payments, home renovations, or furnishings. These loans offer a convenient way to meet financial gaps, especially when quicker access to funds is needed. However, personal loans come with higher interest rates and shorter repayment periods than traditional home loans, making them suitable for short-term funding needs.

Key Features of Personal Loans for Homebuyers

1. **Unsecured Loan**: No collateral is required, making it easier to obtain without having to pledge assets.
2. **Flexible Use of Funds**: Can be used for various home-related expenses like down payments, renovations, or furnishings.
3. **Quick Processing and Disbursal**: Faster approval and loan disbursal compared to traditional home loans.

4. **Loan Amount**: Typically, smaller amounts compared to home loans, as they are unsecured.
5. **Higher Interest Rates**: Personal loans come with higher interest rates than home loans due to the lack of collateral.
6. **Fixed Repayment Tenure**: Personal loans have a predetermined loan term with fixed monthly EMIs.
7. **Shorter Loan Tenure**: Generally, the repayment period is shorter than home loans, usually ranging from 1 to 5 years.
8. **Eligibility Based on Credit Score**: Good credit score and stable income are typically required for approval.
9. **No Specific Purpose Requirement**: Unlike home loans, there is no restriction on the purpose of the loan (besides general legal purposes).

Advantages of Personal Loans for Homebuyers

One of the key benefits of personal loans is the flexibility they offer. Homebuyers can use personal loans for various purposes, such as making a down payment or funding home renovations and furnishing. Personal loans are also relatively quick to process, meaning that homebuyers can access funds without long waiting periods. The absence of collateral and the potential for quick approval make personal loans an attractive option for those who need immediate financing. This type of loan can also be easier to obtain for those who have good credit scores and stable income, even if they don't qualify for larger home loans.

Disadvantages of Personal Loans for Homebuyers

Despite their advantages, personal loans for homebuyers come with some drawbacks. One significant disadvantage is the higher interest rates compared to home loans, which can make them more expensive in the long run. Additionally, personal loans typically have shorter repayment tenures, leading to higher monthly EMIs, which might be a financial burden for some borrowers. Since the loan amount is usually smaller than what a home loan offers, it may not be sufficient for a complete home purchase but could help cover specific expenses like renovations or the down payment. Also, the absence of collateral means that these loans come with higher risks for lenders, reflected in the interest rate.

When to Consider a Personal Loan for Home Purchase

Personal loans can be a suitable option for homebuyers in specific situations. If you require a quick loan to fund the down payment for a home, a personal loan may provide a fast solution. Additionally, after purchasing a property, if you need funds for renovation or furnishing, a personal loan can be a convenient way to meet those needs. It is also a viable option if your home loan eligibility is insufficient to cover the entire cost of the property. However, it is important to consider the higher interest rates and shorter tenure before opting for a personal loan.

Alternatives to Personal Loans for Homebuyers

While personal loans can serve as a short-term solution for homebuyers, they may not always be the best option for larger expenses like home purchases. Home loans, with their lower interest rates and longer repayment terms, are generally more suitable for financing a home. If you already have a home loan, a top-up loan can offer additional funds at a lower interest rate. Alternatively, taking a loan against property (LAP) might be a more cost-effective option for those with existing assets, offering a lower interest rate due to the collateral involved. Gold loans can also be an alternative for homebuyers who own gold, offering a quick and affordable option for financing home-related expenses.

Weighing the Pros and Cons

Personal loans for homebuyers can provide a flexible and convenient way to access funds for various home-related expenses, but they come with trade-offs. While they offer quick disbursal and do not require collateral, their higher interest rates and shorter tenure can make them a more expensive option in the long run. It is essential for homebuyers to evaluate their financial situation carefully and consider alternative financing options like home loans or top-up loans to ensure they are making the best choice for their needs.

Chapter 7

JOINT-HOME LOAN

A **joint home loan** is a type of loan where two or more individuals—typically spouses, parents, or siblings—apply for a home loan together. The loan is sanctioned to all applicants, and all of them share the responsibility for repaying it. This type of loan is popular among homebuyers in India for its flexibility and the financial benefits it provides.

Eligibility for Joint Home Loan

1. **Eligible Applicants**: A joint home loan can be availed by two or more individuals. Most commonly, it is taken by a husband and wife, but it can also be taken by parents and children or even by two siblings.
2. **Age Criteria**: The age of the applicants should typically range between 21 to 60 years, although this can vary slightly depending on the lender.
3. **Income Requirements**: The combined income of the applicants is considered while sanctioning the loan. The higher the joint income, the greater the loan eligibility.

4. **Credit Score**: All applicants' credit scores are checked, and a good credit history increases the chances of loan approval and securing a better interest rate.

Key Features of Joint Home Loan

1. **Increased Loan Eligibility**: One of the main advantages of a joint home loan is that the combined income of both borrowers is taken into consideration, allowing for a higher loan amount.
2. **Shared Repayment Responsibility**: All applicants are equally responsible for repaying the loan, which helps in managing EMI payments.
3. **Tax Benefits**: Both borrowers can claim tax deductions under **Section 80C** for principal repayment and under **Section 24(b)** for interest repayment, subject to the limits set by the Income Tax Act.
4. **Interest Rate**: The interest rate is typically the same as that for an individual home loan, although some lenders may offer a marginally lower rate for joint loans, especially for married couples.
5. **Flexibility in Ownership**: The co-borrowers in a joint loan must also share the ownership of the property, as the loan is provided jointly. Both parties will be listed as co-owners of the property.
6. **Loan Repayment**: The repayment responsibility is shared according to the terms set by the applicants, typically divided equally, but it can be customized based on individual income and financial capacity.

Advantages of Joint Home Loan

1. **Higher Loan Amount**: The combined income of the co-applicants can result in a higher loan eligibility, making it easier to afford a bigger home or a more expensive property.
2. **Tax Benefits**: Both co-applicants are entitled to tax deductions on the principal and interest amounts under the respective sections of the Income Tax Act. This can reduce the overall tax liability for both.
3. **Better Chances of Approval**: Joint applicants with good credit scores have a better chance of loan approval. Multiple applicants can also help balance the risk for the lender, making approval more likely.
4. **Shared Financial Burden**: The repayment is divided, which eases the burden on a single individual to make payments, especially in case of financial difficulties.
5. **Enhanced Creditworthiness**: If one of the applicants has a poor credit history, the other applicant's strong credit profile may help secure loan approval or a more favourable interest rate.

Disadvantages of Joint Home Loan

1. **Shared Liability**: All co-borrowers are jointly responsible for the repayment of the loan. If one borrower defaults, the other is liable to repay the entire loan amount.
2. **Complexity in Property Transfer**: If one borrower wants to exit the loan or transfer ownership of the property, it can be a complicated process, especially if both borrowers are named on the property title.

3. **Difficulties in Divorce or Separation**: In case of a divorce or separation between the co-applicants, the issue of who will pay the EMIs or retain ownership can create disputes, leading to a prolonged legal process.

4. **Tax Deductions Only for the Actual Repayment**: Tax deductions are only applicable to the borrowers who are actually making the repayment. If one co-applicant is not paying the EMI, they cannot claim the deduction for interest or principal repayment.

Documents Required for Joint Home Loan

1. **Identity Proof**: Aadhaar card, passport, voter ID, or driver's license of all applicants.

2. **Address Proof**: Utility bills, passport, or rental agreement for all applicants.

3. **Income Proof**: Salary slips, income tax returns (ITR), and bank statements of both applicants.

4. **Property Documents**: Title deeds, property tax receipts, and other legal documents pertaining to the property to be financed.

5. **Other Documents**: Proof of relationship (e.g., marriage certificate for spouses, or family registration certificate for family members).

Chapter 8

Equity Financing for Homebuyers

Equity financing for homebuyers in India is an alternative to traditional debt financing, where the buyer leverages shared ownership of a property rather than relying entirely on a mortgage loan. This model allows buyers to raise funds for purchasing homes by offering a share in the property to investors in exchange for capital. Equity financing can take many forms, such as equity sharing, home equity loans, or real estate partnerships, and is gaining popularity as an option for homebuyers, especially in an increasingly expensive real estate market.

How Equity Financing Works for Homebuyers

1. **Equity Sharing Agreements:** One of the most common forms of equity financing in India is the equity sharing agreement. In this structure, the buyer and an investor (often a financial institution or a private entity) jointly purchase a property. The investor typically contributes a portion of the down payment or the entire down payment, while the buyer covers the remaining costs, including the monthly mortgage payments.

In return, the investor gets a percentage of the property's appreciation and/or rental income, depending on the terms of the agreement.

2. **Home Equity Loans:** A home equity loan in India allows a homeowner to borrow money against the equity they have built up in their existing property. This type of financing is useful for buyers who already own a property and want to use the funds to buy a new home. The loan is secured by the existing property, and the funds raised can be used for purchasing another home, home improvement, or even paying for the down payment of the new property.

3. **Real Estate Investment Partnerships:** In India, many homebuyers opt for real estate investment partnerships, where they partner with investors to purchase high-value residential properties. These partnerships can be between friends, family members, or business partners who pool their resources to invest in a property. This partnership allows for the joint ownership of the property, where profits and losses are shared proportionately.

4. **Government Programs:** The Indian government offers several schemes that align with the principles of equity financing, such as the Pradhan Mantri Awas Yojana (PMAY), which provides interest subsidies for first-time homebuyers. Although PMAY primarily provides loans, there are aspects of shared ownership and financial support that make it a form of equity financing for homebuyers in lower-income categories.

Key Features of Equity Financing for Homebuyers

1. **No Monthly EMI Payment on Investor's Share:** One of the primary benefits of equity financing in India is the elimination of monthly EMI payments on the investor's share of the property. In traditional home loans, the borrower is required to make monthly payments for the borrowed sum, but in equity financing, the buyer only repays the loan portion while sharing ownership with the investor.
2. **Shared Ownership and Risk:** The ownership of the property is divided between the buyer and the investor. Both parties share in the appreciation or depreciation of the property's value. If the property value rises, both parties benefit, and if the value drops, both parties bear the financial impact. This shared risk is particularly useful in volatile markets.
3. **Capital Appreciation and Profit Sharing:** Equity financing in India generally involves sharing the future capital appreciation of the property. The buyer and the investor agree on a percentage split of the capital gains upon the sale of the property. For example, if the investor contributed 30% of the capital to the purchase, they may receive 30% of the capital gains when the property is sold.
4. **Flexible Repayment Terms:** Since equity financing does not require monthly payments on the investor's share, the repayment terms can be more flexible. The buyer may need to pay the investor only upon the sale of the property or when they decide to repurchase the investor's share.
5. **Higher Leverage for Property Purchases:** Equity financing allows buyers to leverage their funds to purchase larger or more expensive properties than they would be able to afford

with a standard loan. By sharing the cost and ownership with an investor, the buyer gains access to properties they might otherwise be priced out of.

Types of Equity Financing for Homebuyers in India

1. **Equity Sharing (Joint Ownership Agreements):** Equity sharing involves multiple investors or parties jointly owning a property. In this case, the buyer and the investor(s) agree on a percentage of ownership based on their contribution. The buyer may occupy the property while the investor shares in the profits or rental income. This is ideal for people who want to own property but are unable to afford the full price of the property on their own.

2. **Real Estate Investment Trusts (REITs):** While REITs are more common in commercial real estate, some investors use REITs for residential properties as well. REITs pool funds from multiple investors to invest in real estate and share the returns from rents or capital gains. Homebuyers who wish to benefit from real estate market returns but cannot afford full ownership may invest in REITs.

3. **Home Equity Loan or Line of Credit:** This is a loan that allows a property owner to use their existing home's equity to raise funds. If a homebuyer already owns a property with a significant equity balance, they may borrow against it to fund the purchase of a new home. This type of financing is secured against the existing property.

4. **Crowdfunding for Real Estate Investment:** Another innovative form of equity financing in India is real estate crowdfunding. Here, multiple small investors pool their funds to purchase a

property. Homebuyers who cannot afford the full price of a property can use crowdfunding platforms to gather investors willing to collectively purchase the home. These platforms allow homebuyers to access funding that may otherwise be unavailable to them.

Advantages of Equity Financing for Homebuyers in India

1. **Lower Monthly Payments:** Since there are no regular payments for the investor's share of the property, buyers have lower monthly outflows compared to traditional mortgages. This can be especially advantageous for those with fluctuating or limited incomes.
2. **Access to Higher-Value Properties:** By leveraging equity financing, buyers can afford properties they may not be able to purchase otherwise. This is particularly useful in metropolitan areas like Mumbai, Delhi, or Bengaluru, where property prices are extremely high.
3. **Shared Risk:** Unlike traditional home loans, where the borrower bears all the risk, equity financing allows buyers to share the financial risks with the investor. If the property value decreases, both parties share the loss.
4. **Potential for High Returns:** If the property appreciates significantly over time, both the buyer and the investor benefit. The homebuyer may see a return on investment when they sell the property or if they repurchase the investor's share.
5. **No Debt Burden:** Since equity financing doesn't require a regular repayment schedule for the investor's share, there is no debt burden like with a traditional mortgage loan. This can

be an advantage for homebuyers seeking to avoid the stress of monthly EMI payments.

Challenges and Disadvantages of Equity Financing for Homebuyers

1. **Loss of Control:** Since the property is jointly owned, the buyer may have to seek approval from the investor for decisions such as selling the property or making major improvements. This can limit the buyer's autonomy over the property.
2. **Sharing the Appreciation:** While the buyer benefits from shared risk, they must also share the potential appreciation of the property with the investor. If the property increases in value, the buyer only receives a portion of the profits.
3. **Complicated Agreements:** The agreements involved in equity financing can be complex and may require legal expertise. Clear terms need to be set for profit-sharing, decision-making, and exit strategies to avoid disputes.
4. **Limited Liquidity:** While equity financing provides access to homeownership, selling a share or exiting the agreement may be difficult. The buyer might have trouble repurchasing the investor's share or selling the property at a desired time.
5. **Investors' Risk:** In some cases, equity financing may attract high-risk investors who are more interested in making a significant return on investment. Buyers need to carefully vet their investors and ensure that the investor's goals align with theirs.

Chapter 9

TOP-UP LOAN

A **top-up loan** is an additional loan that a borrower can avail of on an existing home loan. It allows homebuyers to borrow extra funds over and above their original home loan amount, using the same property as collateral. The top-up loan is typically provided at a lower interest rate than personal loans, as it is secured against the property.

Key Features of Top-Up Loans

1. **Secured Loan**: Since the loan is secured against the property, the lender offers better interest rates compared to unsecured loans.
2. **Loan Amount**: The amount sanctioned depends on the outstanding balance of the original home loan and the property's current market value.
3. **Flexible Usage**: The funds can be used for various purposes, including home renovations, paying off other debts, or funding personal expenses.

4. **Interest Rates**: The interest rates on top-up loans are usually lower than unsecured loans like personal loans, making them a cost-effective borrowing option.
5. **Repayment Tenure**: The tenure of a top-up loan is generally aligned with the remaining tenure of the original home loan.

Advantages of Top-Up Loans

- Lower interest rates compared to personal loans.
- Quick approval process since the lender already has details of the existing loan and property.
- No need for additional documentation as the borrower's creditworthiness and the property is already evaluated.

Disadvantages

- The borrower's property is at risk, as the top-up loan is secured against it.
- It may increase the overall loan burden if not managed carefully.

Top-up loans are ideal for homebuyers looking to fund additional expenses while keeping their existing home loan intact.

Part 7

Upcoming Financing Options for Different Asset Classes

Chapter 1

Residential

1. Fractional Ownership Platforms

Fractional Ownership Platforms are revolutionizing real estate investment by enabling multiple investors to co-own a residential property. These platforms divide property ownership into shares, allowing individuals to invest smaller amounts and benefit from rental income and appreciation in value. This model is gaining traction in urban markets where property prices are high. Investors enjoy reduced risk and professional property management, but challenges like limited liquidity and evolving regulations remain.

2. Green Home Financing

Green Home Financing is targeted at promoting sustainable living through loans for eco-friendly homes. These loans are linked to properties adhering to standards set by bodies like the IGBC and GRIHA. Borrowers often receive benefits like lower interest rates or longer tenures for adopting renewable energy systems, energy-efficient appliances, and water-saving technologies. The model aligns with global sustainability goals, but high initial costs for green features may deter some buyers despite long-term savings.

3. Real Estate Crowdfunding

Real Estate Crowdfunding platforms are creating opportunities for small investors to pool funds for residential projects. This democratizes real estate investments, allowing early-stage funding of projects with potential returns upon completion. Crowdfunding is particularly attractive for affordable and mid-segment housing. However, it carries risks like project delays or defaults, and the regulatory environment for such platforms in India is still evolving.

4. Rent-to-Own Financing

Rent-to-Own Financing provides a pathway to homeownership by allowing tenants to rent a property with the option to purchase it later. A portion of the rent contributes to the eventual purchase price, making this model ideal for individuals facing challenges in securing traditional loans. While it offers flexibility and affordability, higher rents and limited adoption in India restrict its widespread use.

5. Co-Living and Shared Housing Loans

Co-Living and Shared Housing Loans are tailored for developers and investors focusing on communal living spaces for students, professionals, and migratory workers. These loans target properties with shared amenities designed for affordability and flexibility. Demand for co-living spaces is rising in metropolitan areas, but fluctuating occupancy rates and long-term viability remain challenges for investors.

6. Blockchain-Based Smart Contracts for Home Financing

Blockchain-Based Smart Contracts for Home Financing are transforming the lending process by ensuring secure, transparent, and automated transactions. Smart contracts reduce reliance on intermediaries and streamline loan disbursement. Peer-to-peer lending through blockchain offers quick access to funds, enhancing efficiency. However, limited awareness and regulatory challenges hinder widespread adoption in India.

7. Tokenization of Residential Real Estate

Tokenization of Residential Real Estate uses blockchain to divide properties into digital tokens representing fractional ownership. This innovation introduces liquidity to real estate investments, allowing tokens to be traded in marketplaces. Tokenization is gaining momentum in high-value urban markets, though it requires robust legal frameworks for seamless implementation.

8. Subscription-Based Homeownership

Subscription-Based Homeownership offers a flexible alternative to traditional home purchases. Individuals pay monthly or yearly subscription fees for access to premium housing, often bundled with services like maintenance and relocation options. Popular among millennials seeking flexibility, this model blends renting with ownership benefits. High subscription costs and limited market adoption remain barriers.

9. Social Impact Housing Funds

Social Impact Housing Funds focus on financing affordable housing for economically weaker sections (EWS) and low-income groups

(LIG). Backed by international organizations, government bodies, and impact investors, these funds support housing initiatives aligned with social goals. While they contribute significantly to urban and semi-urban housing needs, returns for investors are often lower than market-rate projects.

10. AI-Powered Credit Assessment for Loans

AI-Powered Credit Assessment for Loans uses advanced algorithms to evaluate unconventional data like digital transactions and social media activity to determine creditworthiness. This method is particularly beneficial for gig workers and self-employed individuals lacking formal credit histories. Fintech companies are increasingly leveraging AI to expand credit access, though privacy concerns around data usage persist.

11. Digital Lending Platforms for Real Estate

Digital Lending Platforms for Real Estate offer instant housing loans via online applications, simplifying the borrowing process. These platforms enable users to compare lenders, receive personalized loan offers, and enjoy faster processing times. Their adoption is growing rapidly in Tier-2 and Tier-3 cities, catering to underbanked populations and tech-savvy millennials.

12. Home Equity Sharing Agreements

Home Equity Sharing Agreements present an alternative to traditional loans by involving investors who co-finance a property and share in its appreciation or depreciation. These agreements provide flexibility for buyers by eliminating interest payments and shifting the focus to shared equity. However, they are still in their infancy in India and require greater awareness and legal clarity.

13. Securitization of Home Loans

Banks and financial institutions bundle home loans into securities to raise additional funding this allows institutions to offer more competitive residential financing options.

While innovative financing options like fractional ownership, green home loans, real estate crowdfunding, blockchain-based smart contracts, and tokenization hold immense potential to revolutionize residential real estate in India, they are still in their nascent stages and face significant challenges to becoming mainstream. Factors such as limited regulatory frameworks, lack of awareness among buyers and investors, technological barriers, and market resistance to untested models slow their adoption. Additionally, many of these methods require substantial infrastructural and legal support to ensure transparency, trust, and scalability. For instance, blockchain and tokenization demand sophisticated platforms and legal clarity, while models like rent-to-own and subscription-based homeownership depend on cultural shifts in how Indians perceive property ownership. Similarly, AI-driven credit assessments and green home financing, though promising, need widespread lender adoption and incentives to scale effectively. As these solutions mature, driven by growing urbanization, digitization, and sustainability goals, it may take years or even decades before they gain widespread acceptance and integrate seamlessly into India's real estate ecosystem.

Chapter 2

Commercial

---

1. Real Estate Investment Trusts (REITs) Expansion

REITs, which pool funds from investors to invest in income-generating commercial properties, are gaining traction in India. While they are already operational, the focus is now on expanding their scope to include smaller commercial properties, warehouses, and co-working spaces. This broadens investment opportunities for retail investors and enhances liquidity in the sector.

2. Fractional Ownership for Commercial Spaces

Fractional ownership platforms are becoming a popular option for individuals and smaller investors to co-own commercial properties like office spaces, retail outlets, and industrial assets. These platforms make high-value assets accessible to smaller investors while offering consistent returns through rental income.

3. Green Financing for Sustainable Commercial Projects

As sustainability becomes a priority, green financing options tailored for eco-friendly commercial developments are emerging. Lenders offer incentives such as lower interest rates and flexible terms for projects that incorporate renewable energy, energy-efficient infrastructure, and sustainable building practices.

4. Commercial Property Crowdfunding

Crowdfunding platforms are providing avenues for small investors to pool funds for commercial projects. These platforms offer a structured approach to funding large-scale developments like office parks, retail complexes, or mixed-use properties. Returns are typically tied to rental yields and property appreciation.

5. Co-Working Space Financing

With the rise of co-working spaces, financing models tailored to these flexible office solutions are gaining prominence. Developers and operators can now access specialized loans designed for shared office infrastructure, which caters to startups and freelancers.

6. Social Impact Funds for Commercial Infrastructure

These funds target developments that combine commercial objectives with societal benefits, such as affordable office spaces for small businesses or green commercial hubs. They attract investors focused on ESG (Environmental, Social, Governance) goals.

9. Flexible Payment Options for SME Tenants

Developers are partnering with fintech companies to offer flexible financing to small and medium enterprises (SMEs) renting commercial spaces. These options include deferred payment plans and rent-based credit facilities to ease financial burdens for tenants.

10. Tokenization of Commercial Real Estate

Similar to residential properties, tokenization is being applied to commercial real estate, where high-value properties are divided into digital tokens representing fractional ownership. This innovation offers liquidity and democratizes access to premium assets like malls or office towers.

11. Impact of Fintech on Commercial Loans

Fintech platforms are transforming commercial real estate loans by offering faster approvals, AI-based credit assessments, and flexible repayment structures. These platforms cater especially to smaller commercial developers and landlords looking for quick and easy financing.

15. Securitization of Commercial Loans

Banks and NBFCs are increasingly securitizing commercial real estate loans to create investment-grade instruments, providing liquidity to lenders and opening up a secondary market for commercial real estate financing.

16. Digital Twin-Backed Financing

Digital twins—virtual replicas of commercial properties—are being used by developers to showcase project progress and attract financing. Lenders are starting to use this technology for better project assessments and risk evaluation.

Chapter 3

Retail

1. Retail Revenue-Based Financing (RBF)

This model ties financing to a retailer's revenue performance rather than fixed repayment schedules. Lenders recover their funds as a percentage of monthly sales, making it an ideal option for startups and small retail businesses that experience fluctuating revenue. This flexibility aligns with the seasonal nature of retail, particularly for segments like fashion and electronics.

2. Build-to-Suit (BTS) Financing

In BTS arrangements, developers secure financing specifically for custom-designed retail spaces tailored to anchor tenants like supermarkets or large retail chains. These projects are pre-leased, reducing risk for lenders and developers, and catering to the tenant's operational and branding needs.

3. Consumer Loyalty-Driven Investment Models

Retail developers are experimenting with loyalty-driven financing, where loyal customers are invited to invest in retail spaces through equity or bond-like instruments. In return, investors receive discounts, exclusive offers, or rental income linked to the property's success.

4. Pop-Up Store Financing

Short-term financing options for pop-up stores are emerging, tailored to brands testing new markets or seasonal sales. These financing models provide quick, low-cost capital for temporary retail spaces in malls or high-street areas, aligning with the short lifecycle of such ventures.

5. Anchor Tenant-Backed Loans

Retail projects with strong anchor tenants (e.g., large chains or popular brands) are securing specialized loans where the tenant's creditworthiness and lease agreements serve as collateral. These loans offer developers lower interest rates and better terms due to reduced risk.

6. Mall REITs (Retail-Focused REITs)

Unlike broader commercial REITs, Mall REITs focus solely on retail assets like shopping malls and entertainment hubs. These REITs allow investors to benefit from rental income and footfall-driven growth, addressing the high-capital requirements of mall development and management.

7. Sales-Based Leasing Financing

This unique financing model ties lease payments for retail tenants to their sales performance. Developers offer lower base rents with variable components based on a percentage of monthly sales. This approach mitigates tenant risks during downturns and ensures consistent revenue for developers during high sales periods.

8. Franchise Development Loans

Specialized loans for retail franchisors and franchisees are growing, focusing on financing new outlets, refurbishments, or inventory purchases. Lenders evaluate the franchisor's reputation and track record, offering loans tailored to the franchise model.

9. High-Street Retail Securitization

Securitization of rental income streams from high-street retail properties is a growing trend. This allows developers to pool rental revenue from multiple retail tenants and sell it as securities to institutional investors, providing upfront capital for further expansion.

10. Retail Infrastructure Funds

Funds focused exclusively on developing retail infrastructure like malls, entertainment hubs, and market complexes are emerging. These funds often align with government initiatives like smart cities and focus on creating modern retail spaces in Tier-2 and Tier-3 cities.

Chapter 4

Hospitality

---

1. Revenue-Based Financing for Hotels

This model ties loan repayment to the revenue generated by the hotel or resort. Lenders recover their funds as a percentage of monthly earnings, providing flexibility to hoteliers during off-peak seasons. It is especially beneficial for boutique hotels and new entrants with fluctuating income streams.

2. Hotel Real Estate Investment Trusts (Hotel REITs)

Hotel-specific REITs are gaining traction in India, allowing investors to pool funds for hospitality assets like resorts, business hotels, or luxury properties. These REITs provide steady income through room rents and ancillary revenue (e.g., F&B, events), making them attractive for long-term investors.

3. Leaseback Financing for Hospitality Projects

In this model, hotel developers sell their property to an investor or fund and lease it back to operate the business. This arrangement helps developers unlock liquidity while retaining operational control, making it ideal for expansions or refurbishments.

4. Green Financing for Sustainable Hotels

Sustainability-focused financing options provide funds for building or upgrading eco-friendly hospitality projects. Hotels incorporating renewable energy, water conservation systems, and energy-efficient designs can secure loans at preferential interest rates, benefiting from growing demand for green tourism.

5. Fractional Ownership of Luxury Resorts

Fractional ownership platforms enable individuals to co-own premium hospitality properties like luxury resorts, villas, or boutique hotels. Owners earn returns from rentals while also gaining access to personal stays, making it an attractive option for high-net-worth individuals (HNIs).

6. Tourism Infrastructure Development Funds

Specialized funds focus on financing hospitality projects in regions identified as tourism hotspots by the government, such as those near UNESCO heritage sites or ecotourism zones. These funds align with initiatives like "Dekho Apna Desh" to boost domestic travel and tourism.

7. Crowdfunding for Boutique Hotels

Crowdfunding platforms allow small investors to pool resources for niche hospitality projects like boutique hotels, homestays, or glamping sites. This model offers developers alternative funding while allowing investors to earn returns from the project's success.

8. Performance-Based Loans for Hospitality Projects

Lenders are introducing performance-linked loans where interest rates are tied to a hotel's operational metrics, such as occupancy rates, average daily rates (ADR), and revenue per available room (RevPAR). This model incentivizes efficient operations and reduces pressure during slow periods.

9. Build-Operate-Transfer (BOT) Financing

BOT arrangements are gaining popularity in hospitality infrastructure development. Developers receive financing to build hotels or resorts on government-owned land, operate them for a fixed period, and then transfer ownership back to the government or a private entity.

10. Mixed-Use Development Financing

Specialized loans are emerging for mixed-use developments that combine hotels with retail, office spaces, or residential units. This model leverages diverse revenue streams, reducing risk for both developers and lenders.

11. Holiday Timeshare Financing

With growing interest in timeshare vacation properties, financing options tailored to such models are emerging. Developers secure funding by pre-selling vacation weeks to customers, using the upfront payments as capital for construction or expansion.

12. Peer-to-Peer Lending for Hospitality Startups

Peer-to-peer (P2P) lending platforms cater to smaller hospitality ventures, such as boutique hotels, eco-resorts, or experiential stay providers. These platforms connect developers with individual lenders looking for high-yield investments.

13. Event-Based Financing for MICE Venues

With India becoming a hotspot for Meetings, Incentives, Conferences, and Exhibitions (MICE), financing tailored for MICE venues within hotels is on the rise. These funds support the creation of banquet halls, conference rooms, and co-working spaces designed for corporate events.

14. Hybrid Financing Models for Luxury Resorts

Developers of luxury hospitality projects are increasingly using hybrid financing models that combine debt, equity, and mezzanine funding. This approach provides flexibility in structuring repayments while reducing financial risk for high-value projects.

15. Long-Term Leasing for Branded Hotels

Branded hotel chains are collaborating with developers for long-term leasing models where chains operate properties without outright ownership. Financing options are tailored to this structure, focusing on revenue-sharing agreements and operational guarantees.

16. Hospitality Focused Venture Capital

Venture capital funds are targeting emerging hospitality concepts like experiential stays, adventure tourism lodges, and wellness retreats. These funds provide early-stage capital for innovative hospitality projects.

Chapter 5

Warehousing and Logistics

---

1. Industrial Real Estate Investment Trusts (REITs)

Warehousing and logistics-focused REITs are gaining traction, enabling investors to pool funds for income-generating assets like large warehouses, distribution centres, and industrial parks. These REITs offer regular returns from lease rentals, making them an attractive option for institutional and retail investors.

2. Built-to-Suit (BTS) Financing for Logistics Hubs

BTS financing caters to specific client requirements, particularly for large-scale warehousing projects. For instance, e-commerce giants and third-party logistics (3PL) providers often partner with developers for custom-built facilities, securing financing based on long-term lease commitments.

3. Infrastructure Investment Trusts (InvITs)

InvITs specializing in logistics infrastructure, such as freight terminals and large warehouses, are emerging in India.

These trusts enable developers to raise capital by pooling multiple logistics assets and offering returns to investors based on usage and income.

4. Private Equity and Venture Capital in Logistics Real Estate

Private equity and venture capital firms are increasingly investing in logistics real estate, targeting large-scale warehouses, cold storage facilities, and distribution hubs. These investors bring not only capital but also operational expertise to maximize asset utilization and profitability.

5. Cold Storage-Specific Loans

With rising demand for temperature-controlled facilities, lenders are offering specialized loans for cold storage warehouses. These loans cater to developers focusing on sectors like pharmaceuticals, perishables, and frozen food logistics.

6. Tier-2 and Tier-3 Warehousing Financing

Developers targeting Tier-2 and Tier-3 cities, driven by the regional expansion of e-commerce and manufacturing, are securing loans tailored to smaller-scale facilities. These loans often feature flexible terms to accommodate emerging demand and local market challenges.

7. ESG-Linked Financing for Logistics Facilities

Warehousing projects that meet environmental, social, and governance (ESG) criteria are eligible for loans tied to sustainability metrics. These metrics include energy efficiency, worker safety, and community impact, offering developers access to lower interest rates and incentives.

8. Public-Private Partnership (PPP) Financing

PPP models are increasingly used to develop large-scale logistics parks and multimodal hubs, with government entities partnering with private developers. This model provides access to concessional financing and government-backed guarantees.

9. Performance-Based Loans for Logistics Operators

Lenders are introducing loans tied to the operational performance of warehousing facilities, such as occupancy rates and throughput efficiency. This model incentivizes efficient utilization of logistics assets and provides more favourable terms for high-performing facilities.

10. Cross-Border Financing for Export-Oriented Logistics

Developers focusing on export-driven logistics hubs near ports or special economic zones (SEZs) are accessing cross-border financing options. These include loans from international banks and trade finance organizations with favourable terms for export-related infrastructure.

11. Industrial Parks-Specific Loans

Integrated logistics parks, combining warehousing with manufacturing and transport hubs, are attracting loans from specialized infrastructure funds. These funds target projects that align with government policies like the National Logistics Policy (NLP).

12. E-Commerce Partnership Financing

E-commerce giants like Amazon and Flipkart are collaborating with developers to co-finance state-of-the-art warehouses and distribution centres. These partnerships provide access to capital while ensuring long-term tenancy and operational stability.

Chapter 6

INDUSTRIAL

---

1. Industrial REITs (Real Estate Investment Trusts)

Industrial-focused REITs are gaining traction as a way for developers and investors to raise capital for income-generating assets like factories, manufacturing units, and industrial parks. These REITs provide consistent rental income and allow investors to participate in the growth of India's manufacturing sector.

2. Sale-Leaseback Arrangements

Industrial property owners sell facilities to investors and lease them back for operations. This model helps manufacturers and industrial developers unlock capital tied up in assets, which can then be reinvested in expanding production capacity or upgrading equipment.

3. Cluster-Based Financing for Manufacturing Hubs

Government-backed financing initiatives focus on developing industrial clusters for specific sectors like textiles, auto components, or electronics. These clusters benefit from shared infrastructure, concessional loans, and lower costs due to economies of scale.

4. Performance-Based Loans

Loans tied to operational metrics, such as production output, occupancy rates, or energy efficiency, are emerging for industrial projects. This model incentivizes developers and operators to maximize asset utilization and reduce inefficiencies.

5. Technology-Enabled Financing for Smart Factories

Industrial developers integrating smart technologies like IoT, robotics, and AI can access specialized financing. These loans focus on tech-enabled facilities that improve productivity and resource utilization, ensuring better ROI for lenders and investors.

6. Industrial Park-Specific Loans

Large industrial parks integrating manufacturing, warehousing, and logistics are eligible for specialized loans. These funds focus on creating self-sustained hubs with shared utilities, connectivity, and worker housing, reducing individual project risks.

7. Private Equity Investments in Industrial Real Estate

Private equity firms are increasingly targeting industrial assets, particularly in high-demand sectors like automotive, pharmaceuticals, and electronics. These investments provide developers with upfront capital and operational expertise to scale their projects.

8. Equipment Leasing-Backed Loans

Industrial real estate projects often include heavy equipment as part of their operations. Lenders offer loans where machinery and equipment serve as collateral, enabling developers to secure financing while avoiding asset ownership transfer.

9. Smart City-Integrated Financing

As part of India's Smart Cities Mission, financing is available for industrial real estate integrated into smart city ecosystems. These projects include shared energy grids, automated systems, and data-driven infrastructure, appealing to both public and private investors.

10. Land Pooling Models for Industrial Parks

In land-scarce areas, developers and governments are using land pooling mechanisms where multiple landowners contribute their land to create industrial parks. Financing is secured collectively, with returns distributed based on individual contributions.

Chapter 7

HEALTHCARE

---

1. Sale-Leaseback Financing for Healthcare Properties

Healthcare providers can sell their real estate assets, such as hospital buildings or clinics, to investors, and lease them back for continued use. This helps healthcare providers unlock capital for reinvestment into operational expansion or medical equipment, while providing investors with long-term, stable rental income.

2. Green Financing for Sustainable Healthcare Facilities

Healthcare projects that incorporate eco-friendly building practices, renewable energy, and sustainable resource management can access green financing options. These loans offer more favourable terms, such as lower interest rates, to encourage the development of energy-efficient healthcare infrastructure.

3. Healthcare Infrastructure Investment Trusts (HI-REITs)

HI-REITs focus on raising capital for healthcare infrastructure projects, such as hospitals, clinics, and specialized medical centres. They offer institutional and retail investors a way to earn returns from healthcare assets while providing developers with capital to build or expand healthcare facilities.

4. Social Impact Bonds for Healthcare Facilities

Social Impact Bonds (SIBs) offer upfront capital for healthcare projects, with repayment linked to achieving specific social outcomes like improved patient care or increased access to healthcare. Investors are paid based on the successful achievement of these healthcare-related outcomes.

5. Healthcare-Specific Insurance Financing

Insurance financing is structured through partnerships with healthcare providers to offer upfront capital for large healthcare infrastructure projects. Insurance companies often help fund the development of new hospitals or healthcare centres in exchange for future payments through patient insurance claims.

6. Government Schemes and Subsidies for Healthcare Projects

Various government schemes, such as those under the Ayushman Bharat initiative, offer concessional loans, tax incentives, and subsidies for healthcare infrastructure projects. These schemes are designed to support the development of hospitals, especially in underserved or rural regions.

7. Impact Investing for Healthcare Access Projects

Impact investors fund healthcare infrastructure projects that aim to improve access to healthcare in underserved or rural areas. These investors seek both financial returns and positive social outcomes, focusing on projects that improve healthcare access and outcomes for economically disadvantaged populations.

8. Corporate Bonds for Healthcare Facility Expansion

Large hospital chains and healthcare organizations issue corporate bonds to raise capital for expanding their healthcare facilities. These bonds are typically secured by the operational success of the healthcare organization and provide funds for developing new hospitals, clinics, or medical centres.

Chapter 8

LAND

1. Land Pooling and Land Banking Financing

Land pooling involves multiple landowners contributing their properties to a common development project, such as a residential or industrial hub. This method allows developers to access a large amount of land without purchasing each plot individually. Land banking, where developers acquire land and hold it for future development, is another option. Financing for these models often involves long-term loans or investment from private equity firms, allowing developers to aggregate land parcels efficiently.

2. Land-Specific REITs (Real Estate Investment Trusts)

Land-focused REITs are emerging as a way to pool capital for purchasing and holding land for future real estate development. These REITs invest in land assets that have long-term appreciation potential. They offer investors a way to earn returns through the capital appreciation of land and future lease or sale income, while developers gain access to significant funding for land acquisition.

3. Agricultural Land Financing

Financing for agricultural land development is a niche option targeting the conversion of agricultural land into commercial or residential real estate. Loans or equity investment may be provided to developers for transforming agricultural land into developed land for future urbanization. This financing often requires compliance with government regulations and land-use changes.

4. Land Acquisition Financing for Infrastructure Projects

Large-scale infrastructure projects like highways, metro stations, and industrial corridors require land acquisition. Specialized loans or funding from government-backed agencies, such as the National Highways Authority of India (NHAI) or state governments, are often used to finance the purchase of land required for such projects. These financing options are typically structured with longer tenures and lower interest rates to accommodate the extended timelines of infrastructure development.

5. Land Development Fund (LDF) Financing

Land Development Funds are specialized funds that pool capital to finance land development projects. These funds typically focus on underdeveloped land or land parcels that are not yet suitable for commercial or residential use. The capital raised is used for land preparation, infrastructure development, and land conversion, with returns generated from the sale or lease of the developed land.

6. Convertible Debt for Land Development Projects

Convertible debt financing is gaining popularity in land development projects. Investors provide capital in the form of loans, with the option to convert the debt into equity in the future. This option is particularly useful for developers who need capital to acquire land but want to minimize initial equity dilution. The terms often align with future development milestones.

7. Land Development Loan Syndication

For large-scale land development projects, particularly in major cities or urban areas, developers may engage in loan syndication. This involves multiple banks or financial institutions providing part of the loan required for land acquisition. Syndicated loans allow developers to access larger amounts of capital, and the risk is spread across several lenders.

8. Infrastructure Development Bonds for Land

Infrastructure development bonds are increasingly being used to fund land acquisition for infrastructure projects such as roads, railways, and airports. These bonds are often backed by the future cash flow generated by the infrastructure or government guarantees, making them an attractive option for long-term land acquisition financing.

9. Tax Increment Financing (TIF) for Land Development

Tax Increment Financing (TIF) is a funding method where the future increase in property taxes generated by a developed land area is used to repay the development costs. This model is often used in urban redevelopment projects where land value is expected to increase after development. It allows developers to access financing based on the anticipated future growth of the land.

10. Special Economic Zone (SEZ) Land Financing

Land acquisition for SEZs, which are designated areas for export and industrial development, often involves special financing structures. SEZ developers may access financing from government agencies or private investors, with the promise of future tax incentives, exemptions, and revenue from industrial tenants within the SEZ.

11. Land Swap Financing

Land swap financing involves exchanging land assets with other developers or government entities. This is particularly useful in urban redevelopment projects, where developers may swap underdeveloped or non-strategic land for land in better locations. The financing typically comes from equity investors or other developers involved in the exchange.

Chapter 9

EDUCATION

1. Education REITs (Real Estate Investment Trusts)

Education REITs are emerging as a way for investors to participate in the financing of educational institutions, such as schools, colleges, and universities. These REITs pool capital to invest in real estate assets that generate rental income from long-term leases with educational institutions. Developers can raise funds by offering ownership stakes in educational real estate, while investors can earn returns through rental income and capital appreciation.

2. Build-to-Suit (BTS) Financing for Educational Institutions

In a Build-to-Suit (BTS) arrangement, developers build educational institutions such as schools, colleges, or universities according to the specific needs of the educational provider. The financing is provided based on long-term lease agreements between the educational institution and the developer. This method allows educational providers to focus on their core activities while developers take care of the infrastructure development.

3. Government Subsidies and Grants for Educational Infrastructure

The Indian government offers several subsidies, grants, and funding schemes to support the development of educational infrastructure. Programs like the Rashtriya Uchchatar Shiksha Abhiyan (RUSA) and the Pradhan Mantri Kaushal Vikas Yojana (PMKVY) provide financial assistance to educational institutions for the creation and upgrading of infrastructure, especially in underdeveloped or rural areas.

4. Social Impact Bonds (SIBs) for Education Projects

Social Impact Bonds (SIBs) are a growing financing option for educational projects that aim to achieve specific social outcomes, such as improved access to education or better learning outcomes. Investors provide capital upfront, and repayment is linked to the achievement of predefined educational outcomes, such as increased enrolment rates, improved graduation rates, or better student performance.

5. Public-Private Partnership (PPP) Financing for Education

Public-Private Partnerships (PPPs) are increasingly used to fund the development of educational infrastructure, especially in government schools, colleges, and universities. In this model, the government partners with private developers to build, operate, or manage educational facilities. This collaborative model allows for the sharing of financial and operational risks while improving access to quality education in underserved areas.

6. Student Housing Financing

Student housing, an essential part of educational infrastructure, can be financed through specialized loans or investment models. These financing options are aimed at developers building or upgrading hostels, dormitories, or student apartments. Lenders may offer loans with favourable terms for projects catering to students, who require affordable and accessible living spaces near universities or colleges.

7. Educational Infrastructure Development Funds (EIFDs)

Educational Infrastructure Development Funds (EIFDs) are specialized funds created to finance the development of educational infrastructure. These funds pool investments from various sources, including government bodies, institutional investors, and philanthropic organizations, to fund the construction and upgrading of educational institutions in underserved regions.

8. Corporate Social Responsibility (CSR) Funding for Educational Projects

Corporate Social Responsibility (CSR) initiatives often include investments in educational infrastructure as part of a company's commitment to social good. Large corporations may provide funding for building schools, colleges, or educational centres in rural or underserved areas, helping to bridge the gap in access to quality education. This financing option is often used for projects that align with a company's CSR goals, such as improving educational standards in specific regions.

9. Specialized Loans for Educational Facility Developers

Specialized loans are increasingly offered by financial institutions to developers who focus on educational facility construction. These loans are designed to meet the unique needs of educational infrastructure projects, offering flexible repayment terms and lower interest rates compared to traditional commercial loans. They are particularly useful for developers creating campuses, schools, or other educational facilities.

10. EdTech Infrastructure Financing

With the rise of online education and EdTech platforms, specialized financing options are emerging for the development of physical infrastructure needed for digital learning. These include data centres, e-learning hubs, and digital classrooms. Lenders provide loans or equity funding to EdTech companies that need infrastructure for online learning platforms, coding schools, or tech hubs for educational purposes.

Chapter 10

INFRASTRUCTURE

1. Infrastructure Investment Trusts (InvITs)

Infrastructure Investment Trusts (InvITs) are a popular financing option for infrastructure projects in India. These trusts pool capital from institutional investors to finance infrastructure projects like roads, highways, bridges, and power plants. Developers or infrastructure companies can list their assets on the stock exchange, allowing them to raise funds while providing investors with regular income from tolls, fees, or lease payments.

2. Project Financing for Infrastructure

Project financing is a critical tool for large-scale infrastructure developments such as roads, airports, and metro rail projects. Under this model, financing is provided based on the expected future cash flows of the project rather than the balance sheets of the developers or sponsors. This approach helps mitigate risk and facilitates the funding of long-term infrastructure projects with high upfront costs and extended development timelines.

3. Sovereign Wealth Funds (SWFs)

Sovereign Wealth Funds (SWFs), particularly those from countries with surplus capital, are increasingly investing in India's infrastructure sector. These funds typically invest in large infrastructure projects with high returns, such as transport, energy, and utilities. SWFs provide substantial long-term funding that is essential for large, capital-intensive infrastructure developments.

4. Green Financing for Sustainable Infrastructure

Green financing is specifically designed to fund infrastructure projects that have environmentally sustainable goals, such as renewable energy, energy-efficient buildings, waste management, and water conservation projects. Green bonds, loans, and equity investments are provided with favourable terms to promote eco-friendly infrastructure development, aligning with global sustainability goals and government initiatives like Smart Cities Mission.

5. Infrastructure Loans from Development Financial Institutions (DFIs)

Development Financial Institutions (DFIs) like the Infrastructure Development Finance Company (IDFC) and the National Bank for Agriculture and Rural Development (NABARD) play a key role in financing infrastructure projects in India. These institutions provide long-term, low-interest loans for the construction of critical infrastructure such as roads, railways, and energy projects. They also support projects that focus on rural development and inclusive growth.

6. Corporate Bonds for Infrastructure Financing

Large corporations involved in infrastructure development, such as those in the energy or transport sectors, often issue corporate bonds to raise capital. These bonds are typically issued to institutional investors, providing companies with the funding needed to complete large infrastructure projects. The revenue generated from the infrastructure is used to service the bondholders over time.

7. International Financial Institutions (IFIs) Financing

International Financial Institutions (IFIs) like the World Bank, Asian Infrastructure Investment Bank (AIIB), and International Monetary Fund (IMF) are significant sources of capital for large infrastructure projects in India. These institutions provide loans, grants, and guarantees for infrastructure developments, especially in sectors like transport, energy, and water management. Their involvement often ensures that projects meet international standards and environmental regulations.

8. Syndicated Loans for Infrastructure Development

Syndicated loans involve a group of lenders pooling their resources to finance a large infrastructure project. This method is often used for projects that require significant capital investment, such as the development of airports, metro systems, and highways. By spreading the risk among multiple lenders, syndicated loans make it easier for developers to access large amounts of capital.

9. Infrastructure Financing Companies (IFCs)

Specialized Infrastructure Financing Companies (IFCs) provide financial products tailored specifically to the infrastructure sector. These companies offer both debt and equity funding to developers and contractors involved in infrastructure projects. IFCs often focus on projects that address public needs, such as transportation, housing, and energy, and provide long-term capital with flexible terms to support large-scale infrastructure development.

Part 8

Key Takeaways and the Road Ahead

Chapter 1

Professional Plural

1. Chartered Accountants (CAs)

Chartered Accountants (CAs) are integral to real estate financing in India, providing critical services such as financial analysis, tax planning, and auditing. Their expertise helps developers and investors evaluate the financial health of a project, ensuring that it is both viable and sustainable. CAs play a key role in structuring funding options, advising on tax-efficient strategies, and ensuring compliance with the latest tax regulations. They also conduct due diligence during acquisitions, mergers, and other investment activities. Their ability to prepare financial models allows developers to present solid financial plans to lenders and investors, which is crucial for obtaining financing.

2. Lawyers

Lawyers specializing in real estate finance play a pivotal role in drafting, reviewing, and negotiating agreements such as loan agreements, joint venture (JV) contracts, and Joint Development Agreements (JDAs). These professionals ensure that all agreements are legally sound, clear, and enforceable. They also ensure that developers comply with various real estate regulations, such as the Real Estate (Regulation and Development) Act (RERA), to avoid potential legal pitfalls. Additionally, lawyers manage disputes related to financing, ownership, and contractual obligations, ensuring that all parties involved in a project are protected legally and that risks are mitigated through well-drafted documents.

3. Professional Valuers

Professional valuers are responsible for assessing the market value of properties, a task that is crucial for securing financing, making investment decisions, and conducting project feasibility studies. These professionals provide accurate and detailed valuation reports, which are essential for banks, Non-Banking Financial Companies (NBFCs), and other lenders when evaluating loan applications. Valuers also assist in determining the fair market value of real estate assets for investment funds, Real Estate Investment Trusts (REITs), and other institutional investors. Additionally, they help developers set competitive pricing strategies for sales or leasing, ensuring that projects are financially viable and aligned with market trends.

4. Investment Bankers

Investment bankers play a significant role in raising capital for real estate development through initial public offerings (IPOs), Non-Convertible Debentures (NCDs), private equity placements, and other financial instruments. They assist developers in structuring large-scale funding deals for both commercial and infrastructure projects. Their deep understanding of the financial markets allows them to facilitate equity and debt syndication, which helps spread the financial risk across multiple investors. Furthermore, investment bankers provide valuable insights into market trends, investor sentiment, and economic factors that can affect the success of real estate projects, helping developers make informed financial decisions.

5. Project Management Consultants (PMCs)

Project Management Consultants (PMCs) are responsible for overseeing the successful execution of real estate projects, ensuring that they adhere to budgets, timelines, and quality standards. Their expertise in cost estimation and budget control allows developers to accurately forecast the financial requirements of a project. PMCs also perform risk assessments and help mitigate potential issues during the project's execution. A key part of their role involves liaising with lenders to provide progress reports, ensuring that disbursements are made on time based on project milestones. PMCs help maintain a balance between efficient project execution and financial planning, ensuring the project remains within the allocated budget and timeline.

6. Fund Managers

Fund managers are responsible for managing real estate-focused Alternative Investment Funds (AIFs), Real Estate Investment Trusts (REITs), and other mutual funds. They ensure that the funds are invested in high-yield, low-risk real estate opportunities, carefully balancing portfolios across different asset classes, including residential, commercial, and emerging sectors like warehousing and logistics. Fund managers continuously monitor market trends and adjust the allocation of investments based on evolving conditions, ensuring that investors receive optimal returns. In the context of real estate financing, they also assist developers by connecting them with institutional investors and helping them navigate the fundraising process.

7. Tax Consultants

Tax consultants are key players in navigating the complex tax regulations associated with real estate transactions and financing in India. They provide invaluable advice on the Goods and Services Tax (GST) implications for developers and buyers, ensuring that projects are tax-efficient. Tax consultants also assist in structuring international investments, such as Foreign Direct Investments (FDI) and External Commercial Borrowings (ECBs), to minimize tax liabilities. Additionally, they handle tax assessments and resolve disputes related to real estate transactions, helping developers avoid tax-related complications that could delay or derail projects.

8. Real Estate Brokers

Real estate brokers act as intermediaries between developers, investors, and end-users, facilitating transactions in both residential and commercial real estate. They assist in market research, property listings, and price negotiations, playing a crucial role in making real estate projects attractive to investors and buyers. Brokers also support due diligence by connecting clients with legal and financial experts who ensure that transactions are smooth and legally compliant. They often have a deep understanding of local market dynamics and can advise developers on pricing strategies that will ensure the property is competitive and market-ready.

9. Architects and Engineers

Architects and engineers contribute to the design and construction of real estate projects, which directly impacts their valuation and marketability. Architects are responsible for creating designs that are not only visually appealing but also functional, sustainable, and compliant with building codes and regulations. Engineers provide technical expertise to ensure that the construction process adheres to safety standards and that the building is structurally sound. Their input is essential in making a property eligible for construction financing and ensuring that it meets the necessary quality standards. Architects and engineers also play a role in advising developers on incorporating innovative, cost-effective construction techniques that can help reduce project costs and improve financial outcomes.

10. Real Estate Investment Advisors

Real estate investment advisors play a crucial role in guiding investors towards profitable real estate opportunities across different asset classes such as residential, commercial, and retail. Their deep understanding of the market helps clients identify high-potential investment options, ensuring that investments align with the client's financial goals and risk tolerance. They provide valuable insights into market trends, assisting investors in making informed decisions and structuring investments in a way that optimizes returns while minimizing risk. By offering strategic advice, they help investors navigate the complexities of financing options and manage the dynamic real estate market in India.

11. Debt Syndicators

Debt syndicators facilitate large-scale real estate projects by pooling funds from multiple financial institutions and lenders. This collaborative approach enables developers to secure substantial loans for projects that would otherwise be too risky or large for a single lender to fund. Debt syndicators manage the process of structuring and negotiating the syndication, distributing the financial risk across several parties. They ensure that the developers can access the capital necessary for large developments, such as commercial office spaces, residential complexes, and malls, while optimizing the terms and conditions of the financing agreement. By involving multiple lenders, they also help mitigate the risks that may arise from single-source financing.

12. Insurance Advisors

Insurance advisors are vital to mitigating risks in real estate projects by guiding developers, investors, and homeowners through the complexities of real estate-related insurance policies. These policies include property insurance, construction insurance, title insurance, and liability insurance. Insurance advisors help ensure that the necessary coverage is in place to protect stakeholders from financial losses due to potential risks such as construction delays, accidents, natural disasters, or title disputes. They also provide insights into the financial implications of securing insurance and assist developers in meeting lender requirements for coverage, which is often a condition for securing financing.

13. Credit Rating Agencies

Credit rating agencies play a critical role in the real estate financing process by assessing the creditworthiness of borrowers, whether developers, investors, or financial institutions. Their credit ratings influence the terms and conditions of financing, as lenders and investors rely on these ratings to determine the level of risk associated with financing a particular real estate project. By assigning ratings to developers, real estate projects, and financial instruments like bonds, credit rating agencies help ensure transparency in the financing process and enable financial institutions to make informed decisions. This process aids in building trust among investors, lenders, and borrowers.

14. Government Officials and Regulators

Government officials and regulators have a significant impact on the real estate sector by overseeing compliance with laws, regulations, and policies. They guide real estate projects by providing approvals for land usage, ensuring adherence to zoning laws, and enforcing environmental and construction regulations. Their decisions can influence the financing structure of real estate deals, as developers often need to meet regulatory requirements to secure financing. Additionally, the government may offer incentives such as subsidies, tax rebates, or low-interest loans to encourage specific types of development, like affordable housing or eco-friendly projects, which can make certain projects more financially attractive to investors.

15. Real Estate Analysts

Real estate analysts conduct comprehensive research and provide data-driven insights into market trends, property values, and economic conditions that influence real estate investments. These analysts play a crucial role in the due diligence process by assessing the feasibility and potential returns of real estate projects. Their reports on property prices, demand-supply dynamics, and regional market conditions guide investors, lenders, and developers in making informed decisions. By analyzing current market conditions and predicting future trends, real estate analysts help all stakeholders assess the risks and opportunities associated with real estate investments, ensuring better financial planning and more strategic investments.

16. Mortgage Brokers

Mortgage brokers act as intermediaries between borrowers—whether developers, investors, or homebuyers—and lenders. They help clients secure suitable financing by comparing mortgage rates and loan options across various lenders. Mortgage brokers streamline the loan application process, ensuring that clients access the best terms available in the market. They assist borrowers with understanding their financing options, whether it's a home loan, commercial mortgage, or construction loan, and ensure that all required documentation is in place for loan approvals. Their knowledge of the mortgage landscape and lender requirements makes them invaluable in helping clients secure the most favourable financing terms for their real estate projects.

17. Surveyors

Surveyors play an essential role in real estate financing by conducting detailed assessments of land and properties. Their surveys confirm important details such as property boundaries, dimensions, and the suitability of land for development, which are crucial for securing financing from banks and other lending institutions. Surveyors help verify property values, conduct land-use assessments, and ensure that projects comply with local land regulations. Their reports provide valuable information that helps lenders assess the viability of a project and determine whether it meets the necessary criteria for loan approval. Accurate land surveys are a key part of the due diligence process in real estate transactions and financing.

18. Financial Consultants

Financial consultants offer expert guidance to developers and investors in structuring real estate projects to maximize returns while minimizing financial risk. They assist in tax planning, financial modelling, and identifying optimal financing strategies for both residential and commercial real estate. Financial consultants help developers navigate complex financing arrangements, including debt and equity structures, to ensure that capital is effectively allocated. They also advise on cash flow management, helping developers balance revenue and expenses, and ensure that financing aligns with the overall financial goals of a project. By working with financial consultants, developers can secure the necessary funding while ensuring a sustainable and profitable outcome.

Chapter 2

Key Takeaways

The intricate web of real estate finance is not merely a backbone for India's property market—it is the very mechanism through which the aspirations of developers, investors, and homebuyers are realized, shaping the built environment and defining economic trajectories. In exploring the multifaceted dimensions of real estate finance, regulatory frameworks, valuation methodologies, and innovative financial tools, this book has sought to illuminate the complexity of this ever-evolving sector. As we draw this discourse to a close, it is abundantly clear that a nuanced understanding of these facets is essential for successfully navigating the labyrinthine world of real estate.

Our journey commenced with a deep dive into the foundational principles of real estate finance, where we highlighted its critical role in shaping the financial architecture that underpins real estate transactions. We examined how financial strategies must evolve in tandem with the dynamic demands of the market, serving both developers in their pursuit of capital and homebuyers in their quest for ownership.

The regulatory framework, most notably embodied by the transformative Real Estate (Regulation and Development) Act (RERA), has redefined the contours of the real estate landscape in India. By juxtaposing the pre- and post-RERA periods, we have demonstrated how this legal reform has engendered a new era of transparency, accountability, and consumer protection. RERA's implications extend beyond mere compliance; it has recalibrated the very trust upon which the sector's long-term sustainability depends.

An equally critical aspect of real estate finance is the accuracy of property valuation and the safeguarding of investments through insurance. Here, we have explored the intricacies of valuation techniques and insurance products tailored to mitigate the unique risks inherent in the Indian market. These mechanisms are not just protective tools—they are instruments that ensure the stability and future growth of the sector.

In discussing financing instruments, we have observed a growing convergence between debt and equity financing models, with emerging tools such as mezzanine financing and government-backed programs like SWAMIH offering a diverse and robust array of funding options. These financing methods are not mere alternatives; they represent the innovative adaptability required in an increasingly complex market.

For homebuyers, the evolving financial landscape offers a host of tools—ranging from home loans and reverse mortgages to fractional ownership and personal loans—that cater to varied needs and aspirations. We have delved into the intricacies of these financial products, underscoring their relevance in empowering individuals to achieve property ownership, while simultaneously contributing to the broader economic fabric.

The confluence of real estate and finance in India is characterized by a relentless drive for innovation, regulatory evolution, and an ever-shifting landscape of consumer expectations. It is within this dynamic intersection that the potential for future growth lies. Understanding the interplay between financial instruments, market conditions, and legal frameworks enables stakeholders to unlock untapped opportunities and contribute to the building of a more resilient, inclusive, and sustainable real estate sector.

As we reflect on the trajectory of India's real estate market, it is clear that its future requires an active, engaged, and informed participation from all stakeholders—from developers and financiers to regulators and homebuyers. The insights and knowledge shared within these pages are intended not only to equip these participants with the tools for success but to provoke thought and foster the strategic foresight necessary for navigating this complex industry. The real estate finance sector in India stands at the crossroads of transformation, where intellectual rigor, informed decision-making, and forward-thinking strategies will be pivotal in ensuring its continued growth and prosperity.

The professionals involved in real estate financing are the architects of this evolving ecosystem, each contributing their unique expertise to shape its trajectory. Whether it be chartered accountants, legal experts, investment bankers, or property valuers, these professionals play an indispensable role in structuring deals, mitigating risks, and ensuring that all stakeholders—whether developers, financiers, or homebuyers—are empowered to make informed, strategic decisions. Their work is not just transactional; it is foundational to creating a more transparent, efficient, and sustainable real estate market.

As the horizon of real estate financing expands, we stand at the precipice of new possibilities. With emerging financial models like Real Estate Investment Trusts (REITs), crowd-funded real estate, and green bonds, the financing landscape is becoming more diverse and accessible. Furthermore, the rise of specialized financing for sectors like co-working spaces, logistics, and warehousing points to the growing sophistication of the market. Government-backed initiatives serve as a reminder that the public and private sectors must collaborate to unlock the potential of distressed assets and create a resilient market for the future. In this shifting paradigm, real estate finance will continue to evolve, demanding innovation, adaptability, and a deep understanding of both global and local dynamics.

Ultimately, the future of real estate finance lies in the hands of those who are not only equipped with knowledge but also with the intellectual capacity to anticipate, adapt, and shape the course of this ever-changing sector. The opportunities before us are as vast as the real estate market itself; it is through insight, foresight, and informed action that we will be able to fully realize their potential and contribute to the creation of a sustainable and prosperous real estate landscape in India.

www.ingramcontent.com/pod-product-compliance
Lightning Source LLC
LaVergne TN
LVHW041144150826
845673LV00001B/65

* 9 7 9 8 8 9 6 9 9 9 5 3 9 *